Living and Working in South Korea

LIVING AND WORKING IN SOUTH KOREA

An Anecdotal Guide for TEFL Teachers

ALAIN HOWES

Copyright © 2010 Alain Howes

All rights reserved. No part of this publication may be
reproduced, stored in a retrieval system, or transmitted,
in any form or by any means, electronic, mechanical, photocopying,
recording or otherwise, without the prior written
permission of the author.

ISBN 978-1-460-92374-0

First edition, first impression 2011

Originally published in South Africa by
Alien House, 2011
ISBN 978-0-620-49501-1

Cover design by Cliff Smith

DEDICATION

For Mom and Dad

For my guardian angels, Eun Shil, Kyung Hee, Jin and Miran

For my guide, mentor and friend, Dr Koo

FOREWORD

Signing up for a 12 month work contract in a country you haven't heard a whole lot about can be a daunting prospect. Add to that the daily responsibility of attempting to teach a classroom full of energetic children who can barely speak English and some would argue that you were borderline crazy. Yet the fact is, that at any given time, there are as many as 40,000 university graduates from the UK, USA, Canada, South Africa, Ireland, Australia and New Zealand living and working in South Korea as English Foreign Language teachers or, as the Korean refer to them GET's - Guest English Teachers.

Some graduates go to South Korea for a gap year after completing their degree, others to fulfil the desire for a new career and some simply seek adventure. Not only do these teachers manage to survive the culture shock of diving head first into a truly foreign world leaving behind all that is familiar, but many of them enjoy the adventure so much that they renew their contracts for 2 or more years with a few even settling down.

Since 2006 I have been part of TeachKorea, an agency that assists mainly South Africans to safely embark on their "Korean Adventure". It has, without a doubt, been the most rewarding period of my working career due entirely to the overwhelmingly positive experiences our clients have enjoyed as GET's in South Korea. Alain Howes was one of our earlier clients and one of the many who stayed more than a year. We are very happy to see his adventure evolve into this book, not only to be able to see Korea through his at times irreverent eyes, but to finally be able to recommend a book that people considering a year in Korea can now read beforehand to get some sense of what awaits them. So if you're seriously considering a year or more teaching English in the "Land of the Morning Calm" then this book is a must if you would like to indulge this adventure in an informed manner.

CLIFF SMITH, Managing Director, TeachKorea.

PREFACE

So why did I write this book? Well, for a number of reasons really. Partly, because I was tired of being asked questions relating to how one goes about getting a job in Korea. I would then end up having to give them advice and information. The other part was for me to be able to share my experiences with as many people as possible. I have learnt and developed so much as a human being having been exposed to this foreign culture. I wanted to convey all of this in a humorous and friendly way. This is why you will find that I have included anecdotes about my experiences throughout this book. Some of the humour in these anecdotes may seem a little below the belt, but I can assure you that they were all done with tongue-in-cheek.

I want to stress that it was and is not my intention to offend or belittle anyone in this book or anyone who may be reading this book for that matter. This applies to anyone, whether they are from the West or the East. There are obvious differences between the two cultures. By me having highlighted these differences, does not make the one right and the other wrong. We just need to acknowledge that each has their own culture and that particular culture is right for whoever is living it. It is not for me or anyone else to judge.

Even if you have no interest in teaching in South Korea, by reading this book you will at least learn things about the South Korean culture. The fact that you are holding this book in your hand right now, tells me that you are contemplating the same journey that I undertook in South Korea for two years. I trust that this book will provide you with all the information and answers that you seek. I'm hoping that it will inspire you to have the courage and take up the challenge of working and living in South Korea.

Should you have your own anecdote about living and working in South Korea and would like it to be considered for inclusion in the next edition of this book, please forward it to me at info@alienhouse.co.za

To view more photographs and get additional information, find us on Facebook.com. Search, "Living and working in South Korea," from the Facebook homepage.

TABLE OF CONTENTS

Acknowledgements	xiii
Introduction	xv

CHAPTER 1: AS A MATTER OF FACT

Fast Facts	1
Where Exactly	6
Provinces and Metropolitan Cities	7
National Holidays	11

CHAPTER 2: THE BASICS

Eligibility Requirements	19
Korean Education System	24
Where to Find Employment	26
Employment Contract	37
Remuneration	39

CHAPTER 3: WHAT TO EXPECT

Culture Shock	45
Arrival in South Korea	56
Arrival at School	66

CHAPTER 4: LET'S TEACH

Team Teaching	79
Classroom Management	85

Lesson Planning	91
Duties and Responsibilities	103

CHAPTER 5: HELPFUL HINTS

Korean Language	121
Health	123
Banks	129
Shopping	133
Travel	141
Socialising	152
Postal Service	168
North vs. South	170

CHAPTER 6: AND IN CONCLUSION

| The Good, the Bad and the Ugly | 173 |
| Letters from Afar | 179 |

ACKNOWLEDGEMENTS

One never writes a book alone. There are always people in the background who help and guide you along the way. I was very fortunate to have such people around. I would like to say a very big thank you to Cliff Smith, who not only agreed to write the Foreword, but also did the magnificent cover design for this book. Thanks to Sean Conradie for all his DTP support. Furthermore, a very special thank-you to my sister, Deborah Howes, for all the administrative support she gave, as well as her ongoing encouragement throughout the writing of this book. And last but not least, thanks and gratitude to Belinda Johnson for all the editorial work she did on this book.

INTRODUCTION

So, you want to go live and teach in South Korea, do you?

Well, good for you! It's an adventure and an experience that you will never forget. I spent two years in South Korea, teaching at a middle school and thoroughly enjoying the experience. Now some people might make many excuses as to why I could go on this journey and they cannot. I want to say that when I applied for a teaching post in South Korea, I was not a teacher by profession, nor did I hold any qualifications in teaching. At college, I majored in Marketing and Sales Management and spent most of my working life in the corporate business world. The old adage, "You can't teach an old dog new tricks," could not be further from the truth. Not only was I an old dog, but I was learning new tricks. You see, I am not some twenty something person straight out of college with a Bachelor's degree. At the time of going to work in Korea, I was forty two years young. Furthermore, the last time I had seen the inside of a classroom was back in my days at college many years ago. If you have a teacher's degree and some teaching experience, wonderful! You will probably find that your transition in Korea will be smooth. For those people like me who are not from a teaching background, it may require a little getting used to, but nothing that can't be overcome. In fact, one of the advantages of not being a qualified teacher is that you haven't been conditioned in a certain way when it comes to teaching. This does allow you to be more flexible and experimental with your teaching style and methods. However, irrespective of whether you are an experienced teacher or not, everyone will have something to teach and offer these kids in South Korea.

The sub-title of this book is, "An anecdotal guide for TEFL teachers," and that is exactly what it is. Rather than bombard your mind with thousands of boring statistics about South Korea, I have included anecdotal stories. Hopefully, these anecdotes will be able to convey more about day to day life to you, than just quoting dry information. This does not mean to say that I will not give any facts and figures. On the contrary, I have included some in order to give you an overview of your environment. I want to stress that this book is primarily aimed at those people who want to teach at public schools in South Korea, although those who are applying to work at universities, private schools or hagwons, will also be able to glean some useful information from this book. Much of the information is of a similar nature. For instance, there will be basic conditions of employment in the contracts, although not similar, they would be fairly standard in covering things like pay, working hours, paid holidays, etc.

I am sure that you will want to do more research after reading many of the anecdotes in this book. It is for this reason that I have included referrals to websites. South Korea has a world class well-developed internet infrastructure that is not only super fast, but also very inexpensive. Therefore, it's not surprising that many of the government departments and services are accessible via the internet. This will enable you to apply for or query things like your Alien Registration Card, Health Insurance, Working Visas, etc. I have included in this book many of those websites that can be of value and assistance to you. Prior to going to press, every effort was made to ensure that these website links were working and active. I found occasionally that a link might be broken or 'dead', but if I retyped the address into the URL, it would then work again. If the link still does not work, try typing the link or key phrases relating to the website into an internet search engine. All of these websites mentioned in the book are available as I have personally accessed them on a regular basis. You might also find that you will land on that particular websites homepage only to find that it is in Korean. The website will allow you to change the language setting to English. The language setting button will always be at the top of the page and usually on the right hand side, although on a few of them the button is on the left.

So how do you use this book? In each chapter of the book, I will give some information about living and working in South Korea. I will then give an account of my experience in the form of an anecdote. These anecdotes will be written in *italics* and enclosed in a shaded table or text box. All of the above has been done in order to give you a theoretical aspect and then followed by how it happens in a practical or real life situation. I have structured the chapters in what I think is a logical sequence of how events will occur. However, having said this, you do not need to follow this sequence when reading the book. You can start with any chapter and then move onto whichever other chapter or topic you want. Alternatively, you can just flip through the book and read all the anecdotes and then come back to the chapter contents later. The choice is yours and it will not lessen the reading experience for you at all.

It was the French writer, humanist and moralist, Andre Gide that said, "Man cannot discover new oceans, unless he has the courage to lose sight of the shore." Whatever chapter you decide to read next is of little importance. What is important is that your adventure would have begun. Are you ready to set sail?

CHAPTER 1

AS A MATTER OF FACT …

FAST FACTS

"Get the facts first. You can distort them later." – Mark Twain

Official name: Republic of Korea

Area: 98 445 km²

Coastline: 2 413km

Population: 48 932 000

Capital: Seoul

Official Language: Korean

Official Scripts: Hangeul

Political System: Democracy

Government: Presidential system

Administrative Divisions: 9 Provinces and 7 Metropolitan Cities

Religion: Buddhism (22.8%), Christianity (18.3%), Roman Catholic (10.9%)

Currency: Won

GDP: $969.9 billion (2007)

Unemployment: 3.3% (year 2010)

Largest Airport: Incheon International Airport

South Korea's economy ranks fifteenth in the world and they had one of the world's fastest growing economies between the 1960's and late 1990's. It has a technologically advanced transportation system consisting of high-speed railways, highways, bus routes, ferry services and air routes. In the first quarter of 2010, South Korean companies Samsung and LG were ranked second and third largest mobile phone companies in the world. It is the world's first country to have high speed fibre-optic broadband internet access to every primary and secondary school nationwide. These are truly remarkable achievements for a country the size of South Korea.

Cutting-edge Korea

These Koreans are really an ingenious and efficient bunch. Sometimes I just marvel at the things they do. They are very big on their recycling. In my apartment I have to separate the garbage or "trashie" as they pronounce it in English, into plastic, tin, cardboard, paper and food waste. Then I have to carry these bags down three flights of stairs and cart them off to the pick-up point about a hundred metres down the road. So I'm doing my bit for the environment. I have actually watched them collect the cardboard. No big municipal truck with a huge crew to help load all the cardboard into the truck. It is just that one person. They sit there and fold the cardboard flat and then load it into their big trolley or onto the back of their motorbikes and off they go. This happens 24/7, as I have seen them doing this at odd hours of the day and night. Apparently, this recycling business is worth millions of dollars. I can well believe it too judging by some of their packaging. You buy a huge box of biscuits thinking that the box will be filled to the 'brim' with biscuits, only to find that the box is three quarters full ... and then the biscuits are also individually wrapped.

The other clever thing that I was marvelling at the other day was the local hair salon. Now I know I have mentioned my haircut experience before. That was where the hairdresser was placing his arms at all sorts of angles, whilst contorting his body into various positions and at the same time trying to cut my hair. It really wasn't a haircut; it was more like an entertaining show. So, being a sucker for punishment, I decided to go back for another appointment. When I walked into the salon, I noticed they had put up a new sign. I assumed it was new because I hadn't noticed it before. The sign read, "... assuring you that we can cut your hair according to your personality." Now isn't that a creative and wonderful marketing ploy. I mean how many other hair salons could offer that kind of service. If they aren't making a fortune from haircuts with that kind of marketing I can only assume it is because it is written in English and not in Korean. Although I must admit, one would have to be pretty self-confident and aware of whom you are before you try it out. After all, you wouldn't want to go in for a haircut and come out looking like a moron or an asshole!

Their ingeniousness and efficiency don't stop there. They really have adapted swiftly to this whole Swine Flu epidemic. They are expecting things to get worse in Korea, especially at the schools. The education department of each province has embarked on massive awareness campaigns and implemented many preventative measures. The other day *my co-teacher walked into the staffroom with this fat, stubby, pole looking thing in her hand. She said to me that they needed to take my temperature. Beads of sweat started to form on my brow, as I thought she was going to ask me to drop my trousers and bend over. Fortunately, it was one of these new types of gadgets that measure your temperature. You just run it over your forehead like a scanner for a couple of seconds and then it gives you your temperature reading. The teachers have to take all the students' temperatures every morning. Anyone's temperature that is above 38 °C is taken to the school nurse immediately. She in turn phones the parents, who then have to take the child to the hospital for tests. The parents then need to give the school feedback. It seems like every day they improve on the process.*

The day after my ordeal with having to have my temperature taken, they all came into the staffroom wearing masks. Naturally I panicked. Where I come from, when people come into a room wearing masks, you start handing them your wallet, jewellery and other valuables! This was just another precaution to avoid getting the virus when taking the students' temperatures. Every morning for a half an hour before school started, each of the teachers spend time with their home room class. They even used this time to educate the students on how to prevent or minimise the chances of catching the virus. I was walking down the corridors with papers in hand and managed to catch glimpses of the video. I always walk with papers in my hand when I walk around work. It's an old habit from my corporate days ... people always think you're busy! The video contained the usual stuff. I got the ones about washing your hands frequently, putting your hand in front of your mouth when you cough, and I even got the one about don't rub your eyes. However, I was a bit lost with the one that said don't pick your nose!

WHERE EXACTLY?

"Wherever you go, there you are." – Author Unknown

South Korea is a country in East Asia. It is situated in the south of the Korean Peninsula. Its neighbours are Japan to the west, People's Republic of China to the east, and North Korea to the north. The country is flanked by the Sea of Japan or East Sea on the east and the Yellow Sea on the west. It is a relatively mountainous country with a temperate climate. South Korea has four distinctive seasons. These are spring, summer, fall (autumn) and winter. The winters can be extremely cold and the summers are hot and humid. The warmer months are from about June till August and during the summer, the temperature can go as high as 40°C.

During the spring months you will probably see many Koreans walking around with face masks on. This is to prevent them from inhaling the yellow dust that is in the air. This yellow sand is known as Hwangsa. The dust originates from Mongolia and Northern China and is swept eastwards by winds and passes over China, North and South Korea, as well as Japan. In recent years it has become a serious problem as the dust also contains industrial pollutants. The Hwangsa can cause eye irritation and low visibility in the air. The colder months are from about November through to around March and during winter, the temperature can go as low as -20°C.

PROVINCES AND METROPOLITAN CITIES

"...ask not what your country can do for you; ask what you can do for your country" – John F Kennedy

How many administrative divisions are there? Why would I want to know how many administrative divisions there are? Well, you don't really. What is more important for you, is who they are and where they are located. The country's administrative divisions are separated into nine provinces and seven metropolitan cities. In each of these provinces is a Provincial Office of Education (POE) which employs guest English teachers. If you are going to be teaching in South

Korea, you will have to work within one of these administrative divisions. In your application to teach at a public school, you must indicate in which province or city you would prefer to work. Normally they will give you a first, second and third choice. Some schools might be in a city. Some might be in a rural area. Some could be in a small town bordering a rural area. It is strongly advisable to do a bit of research on each area before making any choices. Even if you are not applying for a public school and decide that you would rather work for a private school, university or academy, the advice would still be applicable.

Further advice would be to take a bit of time for contemplation as to what your needs are. Ask yourself some simple probing questions. Do I want to go to a place that has a social nightlife? Will it cater for my outdoor sporting activities? Will there be other foreigners in the area? Do I want to work in a city or rural area? Will I be able to be stimulated intellectually? I gave it some serious thought before I made a decision on where I wanted to be placed. I wanted to be immersed in the Korean culture with little or no distractions from foreigners. Being able to save a large portion of my salary each month was also high on my needs list. I also wanted to be near nature where there was a decent place to go running, hiking and cycling. I was fortunate enough to be sent to a town in a rural area, which suited my lifestyle perfectly. However, if I had asked to go to a place which was more cosmopolitan, had many night clubs and was a shopper's paradise, the town I was sent to would have definitely been the wrong choice. I would further suggest that you use something like Google Earth to get another perspective of the city or province in which you are interested. There are many TEFL teachers who didn't give much thought to where they wanted to be placed, resulting in them feeling dispirited for the majority of their stay at their schools.

I have listed the seven metropolitan cities and nine provincial governments with their relevant website address. I urge you to use these websites and do the necessary research in order to make an informed decision about where you would like to teach. These websites contain valuable information about the region. This includes, but not limited to, information on tourism, business, history and the culture of the region.

Metropolitan city	Website
Busan	http://www.busan.go.kr
Daegu	http://www.daegu.go.kr
Daejeon	http://www.daejeon.go.kr
Gwangju	http://www.gwangju.go.kr
Incheon	http://www.incheon.go.kr
Seoul	http://www.seoul.go.kr
Ulsan	http://www.ulsan.go.kr

Province	Website
Chungbuk	http://www.chungbuk.go.kr
Chungnam	http://www.chungnam.go.kr
Gangwon	http://www.provin.gangwon.kr
Gyeongbuk	http://www.gyeongbuk.go.kr
Gyeonggi	http://www.gyeonggi.go.kr
Gyeongnam	http://www.gyeongnam.go.kr
Jeju	http://www.jeju.go.kr
Jeonbuk	http://www.jeonbuk.go.kr
Jeonnam	http://www.jeonnam.go.kr

NATIONAL HOLIDAYS

"All work and no play makes Jack a dull boy." – English proverb

South Korea uses both the lunar and solar calendars. There are between twelve and fourteen national holidays per year. During these holidays most businesses and government offices will be closed. However, large department stores and small shopkeepers generally do remain open. Most of these holidays take place during the school semester, which means that you will still be able to take annual leave during the school vacations, as per your employment contract. During some of the longer national holidays like Seol-nal and Chuseok, you may find that your local office of education may close the school for an extra day or two. If this is the case, it is an ideal opportunity to explore South Korea. However, be warned and plan way in advance. On holidays like Chuseok, Korea literally comes to a standstill as people are trying to get to their home towns to celebrate with relatives. These are some of the Korean National holidays:

- January 1st: New Year's Day
- January : Seol-nal

Seol-nal is for celebrating New Year's Day according to the lunar calendar. It occurs roughly around late January or early February according to the solar calendar. Koreans go and visit relatives and their hometown. It is also a time to honour their ancestors.

- March 1st: Sam-il-jeol

Sam-il-jeol celebrates the anniversary of the Korean uprising against Japanese colonialism in 1919.

- April 8th: Buddha's Birthday

Buddha's birthday is celebrated on April 8th according to the lunar calendar. This takes place end of April to early May according to the solar calendar.

- May 5th: Children's Day

This is a day when children are indulged by their parents and are showered with gifts.

- May 15th: Teacher's Day

Most teachers won't actually have the day off. Teachers from surrounding schools get together and do some fun activities. Our school played volleyball against teachers from schools in the area. We then went for a hike in the nearby mountains. Shortly after that we ended up having drinks and dinner.

- June 6th: Memorial Day

This is a day of remembrance for all of the veterans of the Korean War.

- July 17th: Constitution Day

The Republic of Korea promulgated its first constitution on this day in 1948.

- August 15th: Independence Day

On this day in 1945, Korea was liberated from Japanese colonisation.

- August 15th: Chuseok

This takes place on the 15th of August according to the lunar calendar. Chuseok and Seol-nal are the biggest holidays in South Korea. It is a celebration where the Koreans give thanks for the successful harvest. Korean women wear traditional outfits called Hanbok. They also play traditional games like Ssireum. Ssireum is similar to Sumo wrestling and the object of the game is to unsettle your opponent and toss them to the ground. Obviously the one who lands on the ground first, is the loser. It really is a family day and people go back to their hometown to meet their parents and take time out to honour their ancestors. Seonnmyo is the act of visiting and clearing their ancestors' grave sites. Whilst there, they perform Charae. Charae is a ceremony of bowing and preparing food and placing it by their ancestors' graves. Of course no celebration would be complete without food. One of the traditional foods enjoyed on Chuseok is

Songpyeon, a type of soft rice cake. During the steaming of the Songpyeon, they use pine needles to make the rice cake smell good. And let's not forget the dancing. The traditional dance on Chuseok is called Gang Gang Sullae and is only performed by women and girls. They hold hands, form a circle and then begin to dance and sing. The children aren't forgotten on this day either. They are showered with gifts and money from their parents and grandparents. Many of the stores carry gift packs of toiletries and foodstuffs, which many people buy and give to family and friends. These gift packs often contain boxes of SPAM, toothpaste or even soaps. Teachers also give one another gifts. I was lucky enough to receive a gift pack from a colleague. I never had to worry about running out of toothpaste until way into my second year in Korea. So not only do the Koreans have a truly wonderful time, but us foreign teachers as well. Should you buy gifts for your colleagues? I think this is really dependant on the type of relationship that you have with your colleagues. We are not only learning about their culture, but it is also an extended holiday for us. Depending on what day of the week Chuseok falls, foreign teachers can expect to get as much as four or five days away from school during this period. Remember to book your holiday as early as possible if you plan to go away. Like Seol-nal, Korea virtually comes to a standstill during this period.

- October 3rd: Foundation Day

This is to celebrate the foundation of Gojoseon, which was the first country in the Korean peninsula.

- December 25th: Christmas

Fourteen

According to the Chinese I-Ching, the Ta Yu hexagram represents the number fourteen. It relates to a time of abundance when all is well. If you dream of the number fourteen, it symbolizes the need to commit and maintain focus on your goals. In the Bible, fourteen is seen as being a multiple of seven and implies double the measure of spiritual perfection.

However, in South Korea the number fourteen and in particular, the fourteenth of every month, has its own special meaning. A few years ago the government was concerned at the growing divorce rate in South Korea. I think I need to put the phrase "their growing divorce rate" into context here. Divorce in earlier years gone by was almost unheard of and was relatively low in South Korea. Western countries on the other hand have a divorce rate that can be as high as fifty percent or even higher. Divorce for Koreans is a relatively "new" concept, as there is no real translation for the word in the Korean language. So in order to try and counter the increase, the Korean government decided to make the fourteenth of every month a day for lovers. This did not mean that it would be an official public holiday, but it would be a special day to be enjoyed by friends and lovers alike.

The idea being that on the fourteenth of each month everyone would be focused on their partner and their relationship, thus building a stronger bond between each other. One might say that it is just another marketing gimmick at trying to fleece the public of their hard earned money. However, many of these days just involve being with your partner and enjoying their company.

"If I tell you I love you, can I keep you forever" - Casper ("Get an Afterlife").

As with all things in this life, they have to start somewhere. So let's start at the beginning. January fourteenth is designated Diary Day. Lovers give each other diaries on this day. What better way than to start the year by planning your future together. February fourteenth needs no introduction. We all know that this is Valentine's Day and it is no different in South Korea. They celebrate it just as much as we do in the West, except the girl gives the gift to the guy. March fourteenth they call White Day. On White Day all the men give their lovers candy. In April it is spring time. It is one of the most beautiful times of the year to be in Korea. All the cherry blossom trees are in bloom and are spectacular to behold. April fourteenth is Black Day and lovers, as well as single men and women, eat a food dish called jjang meng together. No relationship could possibly survive without someone giving flowers. May fourteenth is called Rose Day and lovers give roses to each other. It was Henry Finck that said, "Is not a kiss the very autograph of love?" So it's no surprise that a whole day has been dedicated to this very act. June fourteenth is Kiss Day. One is only required to kiss their partner on this day. They say every cloud has a silver lining and so should every relationship. July fourteenth is Silver Day and lovers are required to give each other silver *accessories. According to the lyrics of the Teddy Bears' Picnic, "If you go down to the woods today, you're sure of a big surprise."Now I'm not sure if you will see any teddy bears if you do go down to the woods, but on August fourteenth it is recommended that you take your partner there. This day is Green Day. On Green Day lovers are supposed to take a stroll in the park or even a walk through one of the many woods or forests that are found throughout South Korea. Sometimes we take our partners for granted and miss out on the memories that are happening right in front of us. September fourteenth is all about preserving those memories and has been designated Photograph Day. On this day lovers are encouraged to take photographs of their special time together. The timing could not be more perfect, as Korea is going into autumn. Spring and autumn are the two most beautiful times of the year in Korea. These preserved memories can be looked back upon in times when their relationships are strained and in need of a positive boost to help them through. We've had flowers. We've had candy. So what else is missing? October fourteenth is Wine Day and lovers enjoy drinking wine together. Korea's temperatures drop quite rapidly closer to the winter months. November is no different and it is wiser to stay indoors. November fourteenth is Movie Day. Lovers go to the movies and drink orange juice while they watch. The orange juice is for the vitamin C so that they do not catch a cold. Usually the first snows fall around December in South Korea and the temperatures can go as low as -15ºC. It is no wonder that they call December fourteenth Hug and Scarf Day. Having all this cold about it makes perfect sense to hug and cuddle with a loved one.*

So if you are in Korea, it doesn't really matter if you're young or old, everyone can make their love lives a little better on the fourteenth of every month.
"It doesn't matter if the guy is perfect or the girl is perfect, as long as they are perfect for each other." – Good Will Hunting

The South Korean Parliament Building in Seoul

CHAPTER 2

THE BASICS

ELIGIBILITY REQUIREMENTS

"That's it! You people have stood in my way long enough. I'm going to clown college!" – Homer Simpson

Before one can even think of applying for employment as an English teacher in South Korea, you need to see if you are eligible. The Korean government has laid down specific minimum requirements that a candidate has to have before an E2 working visa will be issued. These requirements are as follows:

- Be a citizen of a country where English is the primary language.

    Therefore, you should be a citizen of Australia, Canada, Ireland, New Zealand, South Africa, United Kingdom or the United States.

- Hold a minimum of a Bachelor's degree from an accredited university.

    You can also have a Post Graduate Certificate in Education (PGCE) or a Higher Diploma in Education (HDE). Applicants who have a two year associate degree or have completed a minimum of two years at university may apply for the governments TALK program.

- Be a maximum of sixty two years old.

- Be mentally and physically healthy.

    Should you be HIV+, have Tuberculosis (TB) or visible tattoos, the chances are that you will not be accepted onto one of the government TEFL programmes. It is a worthwhile exercise to know your HIV status before going to Korea. In the last year or so there was an incident where a foreign teacher arrived in South Korea and after having their medical done, was diagnosed with HIV and TB. Their contract was immediately cancelled and they were sent back to their home country. If you do have visible tattoos, you might want to consider having them removed.

- Have a good command of the English language (grammar, pronunciation, etc).

- Have a clear police record.

    Applicants will have to supply an official criminal record check from their respective countries with an Apostille. This is to satisfy the Korean government that they are not letting criminals into the country. In South Africa, a Driving While Intoxicated (DWI) will show up on a police record. This may differ from the other six English speaking countries.

You may see many people advertising saying that if you do their TEFL (Teaching English as a Foreign Language) or

TESOL (Teachers of English to Speakers of Other Languages) course, you will be able to get a job teaching English in South Korea. TEFL and TESOL qualifications are very similar. If you have only done a TEFL or TESOL course and do not meet the basic eligibility requirements above, the Provincial Office of Education (POE) will not be able to issue you with an E2 working visa i.e. you will not be able to work as an English teacher in South Korea. As the worldwide economic crisis continues, some POE's are also asking for a TEFL certificate over and above the basic eligibility requirements. If you are not from a teaching background, then I can strongly recommend that you do a TEFL certificate before coming to South Korea. This will not only better prepare you for your teaching job, but in most POE's the salary scale is a little higher for candidates who meet the basic requirements, as well as having a TEFL certificate. The TEFL certificate would need to be a minimum of a hundred hours and preferably with a practical teaching component to it. It goes without saying that the qualification would need to come from a reputable training company and not some diploma mill. So do you meet all the minimum requirements? If so, congratulations! You have overcome your first hurdle. Now let us take a closer look at your potential employers.

TEFL

For those of you who thought this particular article was going to be about pots and pans, sorry to disappoint you. Teach English as a Foreign Language. Now there is a misnomer if ever there was one. English is not only foreign to foreigners, but also to native English speakers like me. It can be complex and quite confusing at times. Let's face it, English is a crazy language.

To understand and speak it is one thing, but to try and teach it to foreigners is another. Just take some of the names we give to words that have special functions or do special things. I myself battle to pronounce these words. How am I going to explain this to a foreigner who can barely pronounce simple English words? Now you might be saying to yourself, "I don't remember any special function words that were difficult to pronounce." Try this one, "Onomatopoeia." That sounds like something that should be in the Biology classroom, not the English language. I can envisage a group of students huddled around a microscope. "Oh, look teacher. This one has feelers." What about a palindrome? Yeah, I know what you're thinking! Some sort of place where they keep airplanes. No such luck. Palindromes are words, which, if taken in reverse order, read the same e.g. kayak, mum, noon, etc. Then why not just name them something like reversibles. Easy to pronounce and gives you an idea as to what their function is. Although, this could lead to some embarrassing interpretations. Take the term, homophones, for example. "Oh, teacher, does that mean phone is gay?" It's just not worth the effort to tell the truth. "Well son, when a phone has digits that are the same as another phone and they engage in phone sex, we say they are homophones." Some of you might be chuckling at this, but how many of you thought that an oxymoron was the guy that sat opposite you in Maths' class? What about malapropism, spoonerism, homonyms, tautology, etc, etc, etc. The list can go on forever.

Everything is about rules, structure and form. You can know these things backwards and even recite them in your sleep, but just choose an incorrect part of speech and it can result in dire consequences. Just the other day I was chatting to someone about air travel and the amount of time that one spends sitting around waiting for connecting flights. They didn't seem to be too perturbed about the amount of time spent in airport lounges. They said, "I take my laptop with me and just sit down and play with myself." One's immediate reaction is to tell them that they can go blind by doing that too often. However, one shouldn't really pry into other people's sex lives, or lack thereof. If this well-meaning person had only used the preposition, by, instead of with, the whole interpretation of the sentence would have changed.

Blaise Pascal said, "Words differently arranged have a different meaning, and meanings differently arranged have a different effect." You had to read that sentence again didn't you? However, you tend to know where he is going with that statement. Especially when you start to see news that reads, "A midget fortune-teller who escaped from prison is now a small medium at large," or "The man who fell into the upholstery machine is fully recovered." Let's not forget the unscrupulous marketers. "Don't sleep with a drip. Call your plumber." "Call an electrician to remove your shorts."

As mentioned earlier, English is a crazy language. It can be complex and quite confusing at the best of times. Keeping this in mind, I think I will take the advice of Robert Benchley when he said, "Drawing on my fine command of the English language, I said nothing."

KOREAN EDUCATION SYSTEM

"I had a terrible education. I attended a school for emotionally disturbed teachers."– Woody Allen

Let's start with an overview of the Korean education system. Korea has what they call a single-track 6-3-3-4 system. This means that a student attends six years at a primary school, three years at a middle school, three years at a high school and four years in a college or university. It is compulsory for children in Korea to attend six years of primary school and three years of middle school. The government carries the cost for the students' education in primary and middle schools, whereas the students bear their own expenses at high schools.

High schools are broken down into mainly two categories, general and vocational high schools. In general high schools, after their first year the students may choose their own subject classes for their second and third years of high school study. Vocational high schools offer specialised courses in areas of study like agriculture, industry, commerce, fisheries, maritime and home economics.

Students start at an elementary school at age six and should be at age eleven at the end of their elementary schooling. Students normally start middle school at age twelve and finish their middle schooling at around age fourteen. Students enter high school at around age fifteen and should complete their studies there by age seventeen or eighteen. College and university students start at roughly eighteen years old. You are bound to be asked your age by Koreans. When you give them the answer, they will ask if that is Korean age or Western age. Korean age is determined from conception and they are considered one year old on the day when they are born. To give them your Korean age, just add one year to your current age.

The school year is divided into two semesters. The first semester begins in March and ends in July. Usually schools break for summer vacation between mid-July to mid-August. The second semester begins mid-August and finishes at end of December. The winter vacation runs from January through to end February. The schedules are not set in stone and can vary from each office of education or individual school.

English was introduced into primary schools in 1997 and in middle schools in 1995. They received between one to two hours of English tuition per week. The duration of each lesson varies between elementary, middle and high schools. The duration of a lesson at elementary school is forty minutes; forty five minutes at a middle school and fifty minutes at a high school. According to your contract, each of these would be classified as a unit hour of instruction.

All of the above information should be borne in mind when applying for a position within a Korean public school. A lot of thought should go into the type of school that would best suit your personality and teaching style, as teaching at an elementary school will be different to teaching at a high school. For example, elementary students will be a lot younger and will not have had many years, if any, exposure to English. So the curriculum tends to concentrate on basic conversation with lots of role-plays and games. High school students on the other hand would need to be taught how to write essays and being able to debate issues, etc. Elementary school learners tend to have a lot more energy and will require different classroom management strategies than that of the more subdued high school students. Even if you decide to teach at a high school, you would need to take into account differences between general high schools and vocational high schools. Vocational high school students and general high school students' attitudes and motivation will differ and this would require a different approach to teaching them. Regardless of the level of school you teach at, be prepared for a huge difference in English abilities within the class.

WHERE TO FIND EMPLOYMENT

"Son, if you really want something in this life, you have to work for it. Now quiet! They're about to announce the lottery numbers." - Homer Simpson

There are various places where one can work as a teacher Teaching English as a Foreign Language (TEFL) in South Korea. There are public schools, universities and private academies known as hagwons. Even some of the bigger companies like Samsung, LG and KB Bank employ English speaking foreigners to teach their staff business English or even just conversational English. However, many of these companies usually employ on a temporary basis and don't offer one year contracts like the public schools, universities and hagwons. As mentioned in the introduction of this book, I will focus mainly on employment in the public school sector. I will touch very briefly on universities and private schools or academies and some possible ways of finding employment there.

1. Public Schools

Due to the current economic situation worldwide, many people from the English speaking nations are seeking employment as a TEFL teacher. This huge increase of applicants has resulted in the government TEFL programmes being spoilt for choice. This does have a downside for TEFL teachers. Even though you might meet the minimum requirements, it doesn't mean that you are assured of a job. For example, even though the minimum requirement age might be sixty two years old, they would probably go for someone who is maybe fifty five years old. It also becomes imperative that you complete and submit your applications as soon as possible. In this way you will stand a better chance of being accepted onto the programme.

I would like to think that employment through public schools would be a safer option than hagwons as it is backed by the Korean government. The Department of Education has been allocated a budget to run the various English programmes by the government. These budgets are planned well in advance and should a crisis occur, like a downturn in the economy, there is a budget in place to see these programmes through to their completion. This would mean that a teacher would not have to worry about their contract being cancelled at some point due to financial constraints. In a private school or hagwon, they are heavily dependent on student numbers and the well being of the economy. In times of economic uncertainty, the easiest cost saving is to reduce the employee headcount. I have heard many a horror story of foreign English teachers who are half way through their contracts with a hagwon, only to be told that their contracts are to be terminated because of a reduction in student numbers.

The Department of Education has four main programmes that recruit foreign English teachers. These programmes are the English Program in Korea (EPIK), Gyeonggi English Program in Korea (GEPIK), Seoul Metropolitan Office of Education (SMOE) and Teach And Learn Korea (TALK). A candidate can apply to most of these programmes in one of the following ways:

- Apply online

Applicants can apply online by going directly to the relevant English programme website. If you try one of the website links below and it does not work, for whatever reason, type the acronym of that programme into a search engine like Google and it will list the website for you.

EPIK	http://www.epik.go.kr
GEPIK	http://cge.ken.go.kr
SMOE	http://etis.sen.go.kr
TALK	http://www.talk.go.kr

The relevant English programme website will give the candidate a full description of the procedures to follow when applying for a teaching position.

- Korean consulates and embassies

Candidates can download an application form from one of the above programmes like EPIK and along with the required documents (see website) hand it into their nearest Korean consulate or embassy. It is important to ask the relevant consulate or embassy official if further documentation will be required to be given before the interview. Once your application and documentation has been received, you will then be notified of when your interview will take place. Here is a list of Korean embassies and consulates listed on the EPIK website.

Australia:

http://aus-act.mofat.go.kr/index (Canberra)

http://www.auskec.org (Sydney)

Canada:

http://can-ottawa.mofat.go.kr/index (Ottawa)

http://www.cakec.com (Toronto)

Ireland:

http://irl.mofat.go.kr (Dublin)

New Zealand:

http://nzl-auckland.mofat.go.kr/index (Auckland)

http://nzl-wellington.mofat.go.kr/index (Wellington)

South Africa:

http://zaf.mofat.go.kr/eng/af/zaf/main/index (Pretoria)

United Kingdom:

http://gbr.mofat.go.kr/kor/eu/gbr/main/index (London)

U.S.A:

http://www.koreanconsul.org (Atlanta)

http://usa-boston.mofat.go.kr/kor/am/usa-boston/main/index

http://www.chkec.org (Chicago)

http://usa-honolulu.mofat.go.kr/index (Honolulu)

http://www.houkec.org (Houston)

http://www.kecla.org (Los Angeles)

http://usa-sanfrancisco.mofat.go.kr/kor/am/usa-sanfrancisco/main/index

http://usa-seattle.mofat.go.kr/kor/am/usa-seattle/main/index

http://www.kecdc.org (Washington)

For a full list of South Korean embassies and consulates worldwide one can go to the following website: http://www.southkoreanvisa.com

- Recruitment Agency

Most of the English programmes in Korea have accredited recruitment agencies. It is the recruitment agents' responsibility to source candidates, collate all the necessary candidate documentation and send through to the relevant English programme, as well as driving the whole process on behalf of the candidate. The agency is paid by the Korean government to find and place suitable candidates. If a candidate leaves within the first six months of their contract, the recruiter pays a penalty to the relevant English programme. The candidate pays no placement fees. The only fees that a candidate should have to pay for are those for the courier costs of documentation that is sent between the relevant English programme or Korean government department and the agency. It's a good idea to confirm this with the recruiter upfront and make sure that they don't try and include some hidden cost.

Before applying through one of these accredited agencies it would be wise to check the relevant English programme website for current accredited agencies. It is believed that these agents are evaluated annually and if they are not meeting the required standards, they are removed from the accredited list. Alternatively, one can ask the recruiter if they are an accredited recruitment agency with the relevant English programme. If this is your first time going to teach overseas or first time going to Korea, I would suggest you go the route of using a recruitment agency. You could do the whole process yourself, but why go through the hassle when there are experienced recruiters out there who can do it all for you. The only fees they will charge you are the same fees that you would have to pay if you were doing the process yourself. Keep in mind that if you do the whole process yourself and you don't complete all the relevant documentation, you will incur further courier costs when having to send the missing documentation.

Listed below are the twenty approved recruiters as given by the EPIK website. They are not placed in any order of merit and are listed in alphabetical order. It does not matter where the recruiter is situated geographically, you can choose whichever recruiter you are comfortable with. Bear in mind that if you use a recruiter outside of your territory, the courier costs to send documentation to them will be higher than using one within your territory. I used Teach Korea when I was recruited for South Korea and found them to be professional and thorough. If you're not certain on which recruiter you would like to use, ask them for references of other foreign English teachers that they have placed and I'm sure they will more than oblige.

Aclipse	http://www.aclipse.net
Ask Now	http://www.asknow.ca
Canadian Connection	http://www.canconx.com
DoeDeok	
Educon	http://www.educonus.com
EduVisor	http://www.eduv.org
ESL Globe	http://www.planetesl.com

ESL Planet	http://www.esl-planet.com
ESL Starter	http://www.eslstarter.com
Footprints	http://www.footprintsrecruiting.com
Global Campus	http://www.globalcampusjob.com
Gone 2 Korea	http://www.gone2korea.com
I Love ESL	http://www.iloveesl.com
Korea Connections	http://www.koreaconnections.net
Korvia Consulting	http://www.korvia.com
Oxford Korea	http://www.epikseoul.com
Reach 2 Teach	http://www.reachtoteachrecruiting.com
Teach Away	http://www.teachaway.com
Teach Korea	http://www.teachkorea.co.za
Top Placement	http://www.englishwork.com

2. Private Schools and/or academies

Private education in South Korea is big business. Schools can start up very quickly, but also close down just as fast. If you intend applying for these types of schools, you would be wise to check the financial stability of the school before accepting any position. There are private schools that teach students according to a British or American set curriculum. The medium in which they teach is English. This is mainly aimed at children who are of kindergarten age. Private academies, or hagwons as they are known, were established to supplement the public school system. They offer to tutor students subjects like Maths, Science, Art, foreign language and English. Education is very competitive and parents want the best for their children. By sending their children to a hagwon, they are able to give their kids a head start over other students. This would mean that students would attend school during normal school hours and then go to a hagwon and receive extra schooling. Students can end up at more than one hagwon and learning more than one subject. This has led to much debate about hagwons amongst Koreans. Some believe that it is widening the gap between rich and poor, as not all parents can afford to send their children to a hagwon. It also places tremendous pressure on the children as well. Some of my students stayed at school from 07h30 until about 16h00 and then went to their hagwons for extra schooling. Many of them only arrived at home well after 22h00. My students' ages ranged between twelve and fifteen years old and at that age, it is quite a hectic schedule to manage when you are doing it six times a week.

Hagwons and public schools offer very similar employment packages. The significant difference is that public schools are backed by government and hagwons are not. The fact that hagwons are privately owned makes it very difficult to comment on their terms and conditions of employment as each owner will have their own. Unfortunately, hagwons have a bad rap for starting up and closing down very easily. You might want to consider the differences between hagwons and public schools before making a decision. Hagwons tend to have more than one English foreign teacher tutoring children, whereas a public school will have one. This would mean that you will have company and not be so alone. Hagwons generally follow a given text book which means that you will have very little lesson planning to do. In public schools you will have to prepare your own lessons for your afterschool programme and vacation camps. As there is little lesson planning to do in hagwons, you will be expected to teach every lesson in your shift. In some hogwans, this means between thirty and forty lessons a week as opposed to the twenty two lessons at a public school. At a public school you have to be at school as you are expected to do lesson planning or preparation even if you are not teaching. Hagwons have different working hours depending on the clientele. Kindergartens start at 9am, elementary students at 12pm and adults split shift. Public schools have a standard 8am to 5pm workday. If you're not a morning person, then a hagwon might be ideal for you. If one of your goals is to work off debt while in Korea, hagwons offer far more opportunities for you to work overtime. If you work at a hagwon, you are required to pay tax on your salary. At a public school you are tax exempt for your first two years in Korea. However, if you have worked for two years at a hagwon prior to working for a public school, you will be taxed. If you're teaching at a hagwon and you are attracting more students to the hagwon, then that means more money for the owner. They will want to make sure that you stay with them and could possibly offer you more money or incentives. If security is more important for you than the above, then a public school is the way to go. Remember that they are backed by government.

Should you wish to pursue working for a hagwon, a list of potential employers can be found at ESL Base. If you find a particular hagwon and want to learn a bit more about them, one can type their name into an internet search engine or go to websites like ESL Watch. Alternatively, one could also type in "hagwon blacklist" or "hagwon list" and see if they are listed. The Association for Teachers of English in Korea (ATEK) may also be able to assist you, as they do have members that represent public schools and hagwons alike.

ESL Base   http://www.eslbase.com

ESL Watch   http://eslwatch.info

ATEK   http://atek.or.kr

If all else fails, one can always ask to speak to the English foreign teacher that you will be replacing or get a reference from one of their foreign teachers. There are many pros and cons for working at a hagwon, but ultimately you need to decide what your needs are and make a decision based on that.

3. Universities

It is far easier to get employment as an English teacher with a school or hagwon than it is to get one at a university. These jobs are quite sought after as the university holidays are much longer than schools and thus it gives the foreigner more time to explore Korea and the surrounding countries. The working hours are a little less than schools and in most cases so is the salary. They do advertise for these jobs, but they are quite scarce and normally people only get to hear of them via word of mouth. Many get jobs in other provinces where nobody wants to go and then move after a year to a better location or university. Your best bet is to ask your recruiter or trawl some of the recruiting websites or job forums on the internet. Some websites that have been known to advertise university jobs are:

http://www.hiteacher.com   http://www.eslcafe.com

EMPLOYMENT CONTRACT
"Make me an offer I can't understand." – Author Unknown

The saying should go something like, "Make me an offer I can't refuse," but when you are given a teaching contract to sign you will notice that it is written in Korean, as well as English. In fact in the standard EPIK contract it states, "The English translation of this contract is offered for the purpose of convenience only." Only contracts written in Korean are legally binding in Korea. So here is some food for thought. Firstly, even if you are reading the contract in English, it might have some different meaning in Korean. Secondly, only the Korean version is legally binding. So there is potential for misunderstanding when it comes to the interpretation of the contract. Furthermore, written contracts in Korea are not considered to be as binding as written contracts in America, Australia, Canada, New Zealand, South Africa and the UK. They are thought of as flexible and open to ongoing negotiations. However, if you as the foreign English teacher breach your contract, it is not taken lightly by the Koreans and they may try and enforce whatever penalties are stipulated in the contract. If you are going to work in a public school the contracts for the EPIK, GEPIK, SMOE and TALK programmes generally have standard clauses relating to salary, responsibilities, work hours, housing, performance bonus and leave, etc. It is a standard government contract and has little or no room for negotiation. Your salary is determined by your qualifications and number of years teaching experience. There is a set salary scale which starts at a low of about W1,6 million and goes to a high of about W2,7 million. Private schools or hagwons have their own contracts and potential employees have a bit more room for negotiation.

If you are going to go the private school or hagwon route it would be a good idea to print a sample copy of a contract off the EPIK website and use that for a basis for your negotiation. At least then you will know that you have covered the "basics" and can negotiate on adding other things that you feel are important in order for you to feel comfortable about signing a contract with them.

I must stress though that it would be time well spent to contact your embassy and find out if there is anything that you should have included or excluded from your contract with a potential employer. Your embassy should also be able to supply you with a list of schools, institutes and business that hire foreign teachers and don't honour their contracts. The old adage, "Forewarned is forearmed," springs to mind here. Once you have signed the contract, there is very little that your embassy can do for you. The US embassy website http://usembassy.state.gov offers some food for thought about teaching in South Korea. For more specifics about contracts for private school or hagwons, go to http://seoul.usembassy.gov/t_contract.html

If there is a legal dispute with your contract, you can contact your embassy who will be able to refer you to a lawyer who can assist you. It is advisable to first try and resolve the dispute with your school. Remember saving face for the Koreans is very important and it will not benefit you in the long term to embarrass them in front of their colleagues, even if they are in the wrong. If you cannot resolve it at that level, speak to your recruiter or contact your regional co-ordinator for the programme that you are on i.e. EPIK, GEPIK, etc. Alternatively, you can also contact the Association for Teachers of English in Korea (ATEK) who will be able to give you advice or point you in the right direction (http://atek.or.kr).

REMUNERATION

"One way to ensure crime doesn't pay would be to let government run it." – Ronald Reagan

The benefits in the various government programmes are very similar. As mentioned earlier, your salary will be dependent on your qualifications and years of teaching experience. The government will also pay a rural allowance of around W100 000 to W150 000 extra if you work in a rural area. Generally, you should be on a lower salary if you live and work in a city. A detailed breakdown of the salary scales can be found on each of the government programmes websites. Annual leave has to be taken during the summer and winter vacation and very rarely will leave be given during the school semester. Even if the school has closed for the semester, the foreign teachers still have to come into school.

If there is no summer or winter camp planned for the school, in all likelihood the foreign teacher will sit at his or her desk and keep their seats warm for the duration of the holidays. This means that you won't be teaching, but just sitting at your desk.

	EPIK	GEPIK	SMOE	TALK
Contract duration	1 year	1 year	1 year	6 or 12 months
Salary scale				
City	W1,8m to W2,5m	W1,8m to W2,7m	W1,8m to W2,7m	n/a
Province	W2,1m to W2,7m	n/a	n/a	W1,5m
Paid airfare:				
entrance	W1,3 million	Reimbursed	Reimbursed	Reimbursed
exit	W1,3 million	Reimbursed	Reimbursed	Reimbursed
Leave	18 working days	20 working days	21 working days	7 or 14 days
Severance Pay	1 month's salary	1 month's salary	1 month's salary	1 month's salary
Settlement allowance	W300 000	W300 000	W300 000	W300 000
Schools on programme*	E, M, H	E, M, H	E, M	E

* E = Elementary school M = Middle school H = High school

In the EPIK programme you are given W1,3 million in lieu of your airfare. However, in the other programmes you are reimbursed the amount of your airfare, irrespective of the cost of the ticket. This does not mean you can fly business class! They will reimburse you for the cheapest direct economy flight that is available. According to Korean law, all people who complete twelve months of service (work) are entitled to severance pay equivalent to one month's salary. The severance pay is calculated on the average pay earned over the last three months. This would mean that if you worked a lot of overtime in the last three months of your contract, your severance pay could be more than a month's salary. On a six month TALK contract there is no severance pay. When you first arrive in South Korea, all the programmes offer you a W300 000 settlement allowance. This is to be used to purchase any other cutlery, curtains and crockery you may need for your apartment.

It will be impossible to cover what the benefits would be for private schools or hagwons, as they all will have their own contracts. This is an advantage as it allows the potential employee to be able to negotiate better terms and conditions of employment for themselves. According to the government programme contracts, one is not allowed to do extra or private work outside of their school. If you are found to be doing private work, you can be deported from the country with a possible ban on not being able to work in Korea again. If you are approached to do private work, rather refer it to your co-teacher or school. They can then make a decision as to allow it or not. However, this can be negotiated with private schools or hagwons. Another added advantage, is that you can negotiate with your employer about not having to come to work if there are no students to teach for that particular day.

We're All Going on a Summer Holiday

We are all going on a summer holiday. Well, so I thought. That was until the department of Education decided that all foreign English teachers would do a summer camp during the holiday – with no overtime pay. If you refused, they said it would be instant dismissal. You don't add water to this dismissal because it's instant. With these kinds of terms and conditions, who could resist such an offer?

*So here I am, the envy of many a foreign English teacher in other provinces, preparing something like twenty lesson plans for the **S**ummer **C**amp **R**equiring teaching of **E**nglish **W**ords and **E**nglish **D**ialogue or SCREWED for short. "Really, I don't mind doing this," he says with his right eye twitching uncontrollably, while clenching his fists.*

Okay, so now it's down to the planning. One of my lessons will be on the topic of a summer holiday. After the summer camp, most of the students will go on holiday. I think it will be appropriate to cover this topic. I will start the lesson by playing Cliff Richard's song; "We're all going on a summer holiday". Give the students the song sheet with a few words missing and get them to listen to the song, while filling in the blanks. I will then fill a backpack with a few items that you normally take on holiday. Students then come up to the front of the class and put their hand into the backpack and select an item. They then have to make a sentence using the word of the item they have chosen. So, I'm teaching them listening skills, new vocabulary and by making a sentence, they are speaking English. Perfect. Now all I need to do is find items to put into the backpack.

I needed to go downtown to buy some curtain wire, so I can look for things to put in the backpack for the lesson. My first stop would be the market for the curtain wire. Having walked for about half an hour, I finally came across a 'store' that looked like it could stock curtain wire. It was always challenging when going to the market, because I can't speak Korean and they can't speak English. So it's always an interesting game of Charades and Pictionary! I sensed there was a communication problem. I was asking for curtain wire, they were showing me duvets! This is a market, so these 'stores' consist of three walls with an opening in the front – no such luxuries as shelves. Everything is piled up on top of each other. I had this poor old woman climbing up these mounds of goods to go and retrieve things which she thought might be curtain wire. I assumed she was old. You never can tell with them, because they always dye their hair black. One never knows if they are fifty or one hundred and fifty. Okay, maybe that's a slight exaggeration, maybe not fifty. I think the woman was getting a little tired of climbing up the mounds of goods, because she was trying to force me to take the first thing she could get her hands on. It's amazing how they seem to know what you need even though you know you don't need it. "No, I don't need a steel brush. I want curtain wire." I was also starting to get a little fatigued by all the insisting on taking something that I didn't need. The closest thing we got to that involved curtains was a wooden curtain rod and yes, she did try and force that onto me as well. I almost felt like telling her to give me the curtain rod, at which point I would then proceed to beat her on the head (with the curtain rod) with the pronunciation of each word, No! I...do...not...want...this. Give me curtain wire!" It became quite stressful, so I headed for the chonin store.

The chonin store is similar to the Dollar Store (in USA) or the Crazy Store (in SA). You can find things in the store for a chonin (W1000). I found this little ball that was probably about ten centimetres in diameter. It was covered with a type of cloth and was spongy like a stress ball. No summer holiday trip is complete without a ball. This would be ideal for the backpack. With ball in hand, I promptly walked off to the cashier. When I got to the cashier, she looked at me and said, "Baram!" Translated, baram means wind. Before I could say, 'It wasn't me," she grabbed the ball out of my hand. I wanted to tell her that she couldn't take the ball away from me just because she suspected me of farting. However, she placed the ball on the counter and proceeded to use a small pump to put more air into the ball. Needless to say, my small stress ball had now become a rather larger than expected ball and one where you would need serious muscle power to squash it like a stress ball. After spending far too much time in the chonin store, and making very little progress with the acquisition of items for the backpack, I decided to call it a day.

All of this planning and preparation is far too stressful. I need a holiday. Oh, wait a moment. I've got summer camp instead. "I'm not going on a summer holiday, no more holidays for a week or two..."

CHAPTER 3

WHAT TO EXPECT

CULTURE SHOCK

"My bowl of yoghurt has more culture than you." – Unknown Author

When it comes to a country's culture and it's not Western, we seem to have a tendency to think that it's weird, bizarre or make some other kind of judgment about it. The thing is that it's none of the above; it's just different from our own. The Korean culture is much the same. However, knowing a country's culture and actually having to live that culture are two different things. There might be parts of their culture that go totally against your upbringing and value system or even your way of thinking for that matter. There are things that I really like about their culture. I especially like the way that they show honour and respect to other people. I'm not really a fan of a patriarchal society, but it seems to work for them. As for spitting and breaking wind (farting) in public...well, that's another issue. Like it or not, you will have to respect it. As the saying goes, "When in Rome, do as the Romans do." If you can do this you will find that your stay and experience in South Korea will be more enjoyable and hassle free.

"Doctor Livingstone I presume?"- Henry Stanley

When meeting Koreans that are younger than you, for the first time, you will notice that they will bow their heads slightly and then lean a little forward. Do not be alarmed. They are not looking to see if you have polished your shoes or if there is any money lying on the ground. In the Korean culture, respect is always shown to someone older than yourself. When you meet someone older, before shaking hands, you should bow first. When shaking hands, the younger person should use both hands. Do not extend your hand to shake hands before your senior does. Koreans will give their family name or surname first, followed by their first name. They do this because they believe that the family comes before the individual. When women get married they never surrender their surnames. They always retain their surname. If a man and wife get divorced, the children can take on the mother's surname. Generally, addressing someone "Ms" or "Mr" is used for younger people or employees who are lower in status. Your students will probably call you "seon-saeng-nim." Phonetically, it sounds like "song sang nim." For heaven's sake, do not break out into song when your students say this to you. They are not asking you to sing. Seon-saeng-nim means teacher in English. On your first meeting with Koreans, especially with your students, you will find that they might ask you many questions that you may deem to be personal. Questions about your age, marital status and family background are all asked to establish where you fit into the hierarchy. It is also their way of getting to know you a little better.

South Korea as (un) usual

There is an English expression, "There is never a dull moment." This is so true in South Korea. Just when you think that you've seen or heard it all, something will come along to dispute that. These things can surprise, amuse, entertain or even shock you at times. But that's because we look at it from a Western cultural perspective and not from an Eastern one.

My students will not think twice to tell me, "Teacher has a big nose," or "Teacher is fat." To which my standard response would be, "Sticks and stones can break my bones, but whips and chains excite me ... er, sorry Freudian slip there ... but words can never harm me!" They are not being mean or impolite, that's just their way. The same goes for asking about your age and whether you're married or not. One would think they are nosey little so-and-so's, but many Koreans still follow the traditional Confucian social structure where age and marital status determines your seniority. Personal space and privacy are another matter as well. "Is it really necessary to sit on Teacher's shoulders while reading my private emails?"

I remember one of my first emails that I sent back to family and friends after arriving in South Korea. I mentioned how they didn't flush used toilet paper down the toilet, but rather put it in a basket next to the toilet. That fad still hasn't caught me yet, and I still religiously flush my toilet paper down the toilet. Although this is very stressful because every time you flush, you wait anxiously to see that the toilet doesn't get blocked. This whole thing came about because of the plumbing pipes being very old and not being able to cope with the "load" and therefore always getting blocked. I *also think that farting deserves another mention. It's not a big issue to just let one off in public, especially if you're a pensioner. Old people are excused because it is difficult for them to control due to their age. However, this does not seem to deter the younger generation. When students drop their "bombs of mass destruction", you act the same way as if a real bomb had been dropped and get the hell out of there. You must remember that these people eat kimchi (fermented cabbage) three times a day! Then again, they have a good argument. Farting is a natural body function, just like sneezing. You don't see people sneaking off to have a quick sneeze, so why do the same for farting?*

At the English summer camp last year, there was this young student really having a good old scratch in his "scratch patch". Not only was there no attempt to be discreet, but he was really having a go – we're talking whole hand down the front of his pants kind of stuff. It was so bad that if you had played a speeded up version of the 'can can', you could've added a new event into the Olympics called synchronized scratching! I do think that was the extreme though. Interestingly enough the girls are more guilty of this than the boys. However, it's quite acceptable and no-one bats an eyelid.

As mentioned earlier, there is never a dull moment. Things do surprise, amuse, entertain or even shock you. This was up until recently. Our summer vacation had just started and I was doing some research for my holiday along the South East coast of South Korea. It is at this point when I stumbled upon Haeshindang Park a.k.a Penis Park.

What's wrong with this photo? If you said they are wearing clothes that are oh so last season or if you're a woman and you've dated a Korean man and think this is false advertising….who knows? One thing is for sure, this statue and some forty other statues of penises can be found at Haeshindang Park or Penis Park. This begs the question, "Is it art or is it porn?" The guys are probably saying this is pornographic, while the women are saying it is art. No guys, this does not mean that you can now argue that Playboy magazine is art! One wonders why they would open such a park. Besides, opening a park of this nature seems to be quite risqué and dangerous to me. Imagine taking a stroll through the park and your girlfriend turns to you and says, "Oh, look at that big dick over there." It just so happens that walking in front of you is a rather huge, emotionally unstable war veteran who hears this and thinks you are talking about him. I'm sure he is not going to turn around and say, "Please don't say that." It will more than likely be something along

the lines of, "You talking to me or chewing a brick? Either way you are going to lose your teeth!"
  So, am I surprised? Am I shocked? Am I amused? Am I entertained? The jury is still out on this one. However, I'm sure that just around the corner there is another instalment to my Korean adventure to ensure that there is never a dull moment!

"You can tell a lot about a fellow's character by his way of eating jellybeans." – Ronald Reagan

Going to a Korean restaurant for the first time is quite an experience. The first thing you will notice is that you will have to remove your shoes before entering the eating area. The second thing is that there are no chairs to sit on and the tables are very low. You will end up sitting on a cushion on the floor, cross-legged for the duration of the meal. Furthermore, if you don't know how to use chopsticks, now would be a good time to learn. If you are new to chopsticks, learn to use them with your right hand. I am left-handed, which seems to be a rarity in South Korea I might add, and therefore learned to use the chopsticks with my left hand. This does become awkward when eating in a restaurant or school canteen, as all the Koreans eat with their right hand and you tend to bump each other when you eat. It is not good etiquette to stick ones chopsticks into your rice. This symbolises that the food is reserved for the dead. Rather place the chopsticks next to the bowl on the table or lay them across the top of the rice bowl. Please note that not all the restaurants that you come across will be like the ones described above, there will be others that cater for Westerners by having tables and chairs, and knives and forks to boot. Generally people wait for the eldest or most senior person to start eating before they start eating. Unlike Westerners, Koreans eat communally. They believe that the sharing brings one closer and is often the basis for building better relationships. Everyone has their own bowl of rice, but everything else is placed in separate dishes in the centre of the table for everyone to share. For example, this would mean that everyone will dip their spoon into a communal soup and continue to do so until the soup is finished. Many foreigners are freaked out by this as they believe this to be unhygienic. My take on this, "What doesn't kill you makes you fat." Initially my co-teachers used to automatically serve up a side dish of everything for me, but that didn't last long as I was quite happy to eat according to their custom. So if you really are appalled by having to share your meal, ask them very politely if you may have your own side dish of whatever they are sharing. They tend to understand that foreigners are a bit wary of sharing in this way. Once the meal is finished people tend to wait for everyone to finish before leaving the table.

"Hands that give also receive."- Author Unknown

When you pass or receive something it is good manners to observe this rule. If the person is of a higher social stature or older than you, they will pass the object to you using only one hand. You would then receive the object with one hand, whilst placing the other hand under the arm that is receiving the object. In other words, the hand must support the arm that is receiving the object. How far up or down the arm the hand needs to be, depends on the seniority of the person. For example, a person who is a few years older than you, you would touch the arm with your hand just above the wrist. Someone like your principal who is more senior than you, your hand would touch the arm closer to the armpit. Alternatively, it is also quite acceptable for the junior person to use both hands when accepting something. You will find that when your students pass you a document or some object, they will do so with both hands. It is also not uncommon to see people who are not familiar with each other, to give and receive items with both hands.

"Everyone should believe in something. I believe I will have another drink." - Unknown

Drinking is worth a mention here, as it plays such a big role in the Korean culture. Just as sharing a communal meal builds relationships, so does sharing a drink. You will find at social gatherings that your colleagues will come around with a small (shot) glass and offer you soju. Soju is traditionally made from rice and tastes a little like Vodka. It varies in alcohol content from anywhere between twenty and forty percent. Offering you a drink from their glass is their way of showing that they want to build a good relationship with you. If the thought of having to drink out of the same glass as everyone else unsettles you, then politely ask if you can use your own cup or glass. Remember, soju contains at least twenty percent alcohol. No germs will stand a chance. Once your colleague has poured you a drink, it is polite to turn your head away from them. It is also polite for a woman to place their hand over the glass and their mouth when downing the drink. Once you have downed the drink, return the glass back to the person and offer to pour them one. You should use both hands when pouring a drink for your colleague. It is rude to refuse a drink. If you don't drink alcohol, rather ask them to pour you a shot of coco-cola, cider or whatever else you are drinking at the time. This way you will not offend anyone and you would still be building a friendship with them. If there is only one thing you can remember about Korean drinking etiquette, let it be this, "Always keep your seniors' glass full."

"Much ado about nothing" – William Shakespeare

You will also encounter some behaviour which you might think is a little out of place, from a Westerner's perspective that is. It is not unheard of to see two grown men walking down the road hand-in-hand. I had many boy students holding each other's hands or sitting on each other's laps during class time. Even at the gym in the showers, you will see a man washing or scrubbing another man's back. This does not mean they are homosexual. That is just how they act towards their friends. During your class time with your students, you will probably encounter students who are continually grooming their appearances by looking into their hand-held mirrors. It's normal, even though you will notice that the boys are doing it more than the girls! It would seem that all and sundry have the need to spit and everywhere you go you'll find people doing it. It's not always silent either. Some sound like a car trying to start on a cold morning and have to go on about a two minute build up before doing the actual act of spitting. My only advice to you is to shut-off from it and to watch where you walk. The other little bug bear that you might have is one of personal space. What personal space? If you are standing in a queue, make sure you're standing right up to the person in front of you. If not, it's quite possible that someone could squeeze in ahead of you. If they see a gap in a queue, they assume that you aren't waiting in the line. Don't be taken aback if you're on a train or bus and someone throws their bag on a seat that you were about to take. This is considered rude in Korean society, but it happens. You will also be bumped and pushed in open spaces. No use in getting worked up about it. Accept it and just move on. A friend of mine who worked at a school on the border of North and South Korea had a rather interesting event happen to her regarding personal privacy. When she came back into the staff room after teaching her class, she found that the teachers had read her email from her mother and were discussing it amongst themselves. In the West, we would find this behaviour to be an invasion of privacy. However, they see it as looking out for you and wanting to help you with problems you might have. They are very family orientated and they will see you as part of that family. Keep in mind that it is more important for them to have the group's interest at heart before that of the individual. If you can't change your situation, then change your attitude. There will be times when you feel yourself starting to become a little overwhelmed by it all. When this happens, SMILE! Koreans love people who smile and many a difficult situation can be dissolved with a smile.

Whether you like or dislike their culture, if you are open to it, you will find that the Koreans will have a lot to teach you. They are fiercely patriotic with an abundance of compassion, sharing, kindness and generosity to give. Once you have formed a friendship with them, it will be very difficult to break that friendship.

Compassion

The last few days in South Korea have been rather interesting to say the least. North Korea has again been testing their nuclear weapons, which has put South Korea's military on high alert. Furthermore, one of South Korea's much loved former Presidents, Roh Moo-hyun, committed suicide over the weekend.

Last week he was questioned for hours by prosecutors about $6 million that was given to his family by a Seoul businessman. This businessman had been implicated in a number of bribery scandals. The press was speculating that the former president was going to be charged, and that it was just the level of severity of the charge that the prosecutors were still to decide upon. Mr Roh Moo-hyun had killed himself by jumping off a rocky cliff near his home. He left a suicide note saying that he didn't want to be a burden to others for the rest of his life and that people must not be too sad or feel sorry. He also asked people not to blame anybody.

I was in Seoul when the news broke. Everywhere where there was a TV, people were huddled around to watch. You could see the disbelief and absolute shock on their faces. The TV showed pictures from all over South Korea. Many people were crying, while others wanted to collapse onto the ground if it were not for the people around them holding them up. The government has set up areas throughout the country where people can go and pay their last respects to the former president.

Even my colleagues at school were deeply affected by the news. One teacher told me how she cried when she heard the news. She cried the following day as well. When she asked some of the students how they felt, not many had paid much attention to the news. Of course, this upset her even more and she wanted to cry again because of the students' lack of respect. Another colleague was also angry at some of his students because they had not gone and paid their last respects to the former president. Many of my colleagues see this as students being selfish.

Through all of this, it would seem that no-one is really interested in whether the former president is guilty of bribery or not. All of that does not matter. They have lost someone they have loved and there is nothing more than a huge outpouring of compassion.

"Have compassion for all beings, rich and poor alike; each has their suffering. Some suffer too much, others too little." – Buddha.

ARRIVAL IN SOUTH KOREA

"Houston. Tranquillity Base here. The eagle has landed." – Neil Armstrong

Welcome to Incheon Airport, South Korea! Incheon Airport is located some 70km west of Seoul. In terms of passengers, it is the eighth busiest airport in the world. It has received a five star rating from Skytrax and has been voted best airport by the Airports Council International (ACI) for five consecutive years. So now you know.

To the seasoned traveller an explanation on how to get from the plane to the arrivals hall might seem a bit anal retentive. For those that have never travelled outside of their home town never mind overseas, this could be quite an anxious experience. When you disembark from your flight you will end up on the second floor of the concourse building and will have to pass through quarantine. Here passengers pass through an infrared thermal image camera one by one. Once the authorities have established that you are not carrying anything infectious, except your passion for teaching English that is, you will then move towards the escalators. Take the escalators down to the first floor and catch the first available shuttle train to the passenger terminal. Don't be too concerned if you arrive there and you have missed the train. The shuttle trains run between the terminals and concourse every five minutes. Once in the passenger terminal, you will be required to go through Immigration. It's a good idea to keep a signed copy of your teaching contract at hand. For some or other reason for my initial one year teaching contract I was asked to show them a copy. For my second year of teaching they did not seem to bother. From Immigration you will then move to Baggage Collection to get your luggage. Once you have received your luggage you will be required to go through Customs Inspection. Besides marijuana and other illicit drugs, if you are not sure what else needs to be declared at customs, ask your travel agent for advice or go to the Incheon Airport website.

Once you have cleared customs, you will then enter into the Arrivals Hall. In all likelihood there will be someone at the

Arrivals Hall to meet you. If you are on a programme like EPIK, they will have a designated counter at arrivals and you can ask someone to point you in that direction. Furthermore, if your contract starts at the beginning of the March or August semester there will be more than three hundred of you arriving in Korea at the same time. So there is no need to panic alone. At least a handful should know in which direction to go. If like me, you are starting your contract mid-semester, you won't have the benefit of relying on the crowd. However, if your recruiter is worth their salt, they would have arranged someone to meet you at the airport. They would have also given you Korean telephone numbers to contact in case of emergencies or in need of assistance.

Those teachers that arrive at the start of each semester will go straight from the airport to a teachers' orientation programme. These orientation programmes can last from anything between three days to a whole week. They are extremely beneficial as it gives you an opportunity to be exposed to what your living and working life will actually be like in Korea. It is also an excellent opportunity to network with other teachers and form friendships that will last for years to come. After your orientation period, you will then be sent to your respective province or city to take up your duties at your school/s.

For those of you that are starting your contract mid-semester, you will more than likely not attend the orientation programme immediately. This would mean that you will go directly from the airport to your province or city where you will work. When I arrived at Incheon Airport my recruiter had arranged for someone to meet me at the airport. I was driven to the main bus terminal in Seoul, where I caught a bus to the province in which I was going to work. It was only about two weeks later that I was lucky enough to attend a three day orientation program in Seoul. I believe that foreigners who are on the GEPIK programme have to wait for almost three months before they attend an orientation.

Irrespective of whether someone has arranged to meet you at the airport or not, it can do no harm to familiarise yourself with your surroundings. The Incheon Airport website has tons of useful information on it. The Airport Guide can be downloaded from the website and could prove to be invaluable to the first time visitor. The guide contains information on customs declaration, transportation services, airport maps and other useful information. To view the website go to: http://www.airport.kr/eng

Whether you arrive at the beginning of the semester or during mid-semester, at some point you are going to be sent to your province or city for the first time. Most of the contracts stipulate that the foreign teacher is to be given a settlement allowance of a certain amount of money. This allowance is meant to be used to buy any further crockery, cutlery and foodstuffs to see you through until your first pay day. It is a good idea to bring a little extra of your own money for emergencies. The government programmes recommend taking the equivalent of between $750 and a $1000. Once you've arrived in your town or city, one of the first things your co-teacher will do, is to take you to buy some foodstuffs for your apartment. Unless you are an expert on Korean food, I would rather stick to the basics like tea, coffee, milk, bread, cereals fruit, vegetables, etc. Once you are settled in you can start to explore all the other alternatives available.

Your co-teacher will also take you to your apartment. If you're on a programme like EPIK, GEPIK, SMOE or even TALK, the contracts are pretty standard as to the type of accommodation you can expect. The contract will also state whether it comes fully furnished and with what appliances. If they do supply you with cutlery and crockery, it will be very minimal and in all likelihood, you will have to go out and purchase more. For single foreign teachers you will be given a one roomed apartment. A one roomed apartment is just that one room. Obviously the ablution facilities are separate, but the rest of the living area is all enclosed in that one room. It's not unheard of that they may give you something bigger. In my first year of teaching, I was given a lovely three roomed apartment, but in my second year I reverted to a one roomed apartment. If you are lucky you may get a bath in your bathroom. Most of the one roomed apartments have a toilet, washbasin and a hand-held shower in the bathroom. The shower area is not demarcated and when you shower the whole bathroom area gets wet, including the walls, floors and even the toilet. For foreign teachers that will have their partners with them, they are usually assigned a two roomed apartment or bigger. Sometimes foreigners have complained of their apartment being mouldy or in a bad area. If this happens to you, it's best to discuss this with your co-teacher and hopefully they can resolve this for you. Do not be alarmed if you arrive at your apartment to find it in a filthy state. The previous foreign teacher or tenant may have conveniently forgotten to clean it before they left. No use complaining. Reach for the rubber gloves, scrubbing brush and detergents and start cleaning.

One of the first things that you will notice when entering your apartment is that your co-teacher will remove their shoes. This is their custom in Korea. Many Koreans sleep on the floor, as well as eat while sitting on the floor. They believe it is unhygienic to walk inside your apartment with shoes on and it is for this reason that they remove their shoes. I had three pairs of indoor slippers in my apartment. I used one pair to walk around in the living area, one pair to use in the bathroom area and the other pair to use to walk on the balcony. Another little point you might want to remember or maybe not. In Korea, they do not flush the used toilet paper down the toilet. They place the used toilet paper in a basket or bin beside the toilet. Once this basket is filled, it is emptied into a plastic bag and put out with the garbage. No, no one does it for you; you have to do it yourself.

The electricity voltage is 220V compatible. The electricity wall sockets only take the two-pronged type of plugs. Some countries like South Africa use the three-pronged round plug. If your electrical appliances are a 100V and/or only have a three-pronged plug on them, voltage and plug adapters can be purchased at local stores. They say that the Korean tap water is safe to drink, but if you prefer to drink bottled water, it is widely available and relatively inexpensive. Your apartment will come with under floor heating and is generally powered by gas. A word of caution about the use of your under floor heating. During the winter months there will be the temptation to have the heating on all the time and this will increase the cost of your living expenses as the gas consumption is quite high. When you initially use the under floor heating, I would monitor how often and for how long you are using it each time. When your bill arrives at the end of the month you will be able to gauge how expensive or inexpensive it is. You can then decide on how often or how little you want to use it in the future. Don't be alarmed if you get a knock at your door at odd hours of the day. There are inspectors that do regular checks in apartments for gas leaks at all times of the day and night. Every month you will also be sent utility bills for things like your internet, telephone, gas, electricity, etc. These bills can either be paid via a deduction from your bank account or you can take the utility bill to the bank and pay it there.

Landlords and Other Fine Occupations

Some strange things have been happening in my apartment lately. For one thing, my bathroom light has been playing up. Every time I try and put the light on, it goes on for a brief second and then goes off again. When I put the extractor fan on, the light mysteriously comes on for another brief second and then it goes off again. The other thing that I have noticed, especially in the kitchen, are things that I can see darting or scurrying away from out of the corner of my eye. Upon further investigation I don't seem to find anything. Now I'm not for one moment suggesting that I have poltergeists, ghosts or anything else that might be classified as paranormal activity in my apartment. Although, sometimes when I hear those blood curdling cries from my neighbours below I begin to wonder. But these things are strange all the same.

Having project managed the building of my own home, I have a little experience in doing some home maintenance or repairs. In fact, just the other day my toilet became blocked and I was contemplating having to call the landlord. The only problem is that I had not figured out how I was going to explain the toilet paper in the toilet. I had broken out into a cold sweat and was frantically plunging away, using a toilet brush as a plunger, in the hope that I could clear the blockage. I was even prepared to try affirmations, power of positive thinking, prayer, you name it. I would have tried anything to clear the blockage. Fortunately, the Gods were smiling on me, because after several "flushes" and further frantic plunging, the toilet miraculously cleared itself and the water went down to an acceptable level...just below, "It's time to get out your life raft." I know this should be a lesson to me and that from now on I should place the toilet paper in the bin instead of flushing it, but I'm sorry old habits die hard!

So based on my wealth of maintenance experience, it would seem that my bathroom light must be a loose connection and can't possibly be a fused bulb, otherwise it wouldn't come on. As for the darting and scurrying that I'm seeing out of the corner of my eye, well that must certainly be cockroaches. Under normal circumstances I would try and do the repairs myself, but when it comes to electricity, I will rather let the experts do the job. The cockroach infestation is another thing. When it comes to buying insect repellent or poison in Korea I am a bit hesitant. Everything is quite potent. They upgraded our English room earlier this year and we are still getting headaches from the paint and glue fumes. I suppose that would also explain some of the bizarre behaviour that goes on in the classroom. I don't want to go and buy some cockroach spray or poison and find that after spraying it in my apartment, about a week later I start to grow a third nipple or something. Looks like I will have to get the opinion and help of my co-teacher again.

I explained the problems to my co-teacher and asked if she would contact the landlord and let him know about the issues in my apartment. The issues of the bathroom light and cockroaches, not the poltergeists, in case you were wondering. My co-teacher seems to always start to give her advice with a question, "You know what you should do?" I'm not sure why she does this, as clearly I would not ask her if I did know what to do! She suggested that I catch a cockroach, tie it up, torture it and then let it go. By doing this, the cockroach will then go and tell all the other cockroaches and then they will leave my apartment. I smiled politely. I felt like going home and catching a few cockroaches and putting them in her handbag and watch from a distance as the fun begins. She started with her rhetorical questions again, "Do you know what cockroaches are afraid of?" Then went into 'charades mode' and started making the motion as if she was brushing her teeth. I must have had a momentary lapse of sanity because I answered, "Teeth!" Well, I thought it would be a logical answer because why would they be afraid of people brushing their teeth? It turns out cockroaches, well at least Korean cockroaches, are afraid of tooth paste. The advice was to put some toothpaste into a spray bottle with water and spray the cockroaches. This apparently kills them. This makes me wonder what the hell is in the Korean toothpaste! We agreed to leave all the issues up to the expert and decided to call the landlord.

When I arrived home that evening the landlord was already waiting for me at my apartment. I showed him the 'haunted' light switch in the bathroom. I also pointed out all the dead cockroach bodies as evidence of a cockroach infestation. He immediately went into the bathroom and started working on the light. No holy water or exorcism was needed to fix the light, just a new light bulb. My ego and reputation as a handyman had taken a serious knock. So much for my loose wire theory! He then proceeded to explain that the cockroaches were coming from the restaurant that was two floors below my apartment. Obviously they were tired of restaurant food and wanted a home-cooked meal. I can't think of any other reason why they would want to climb two floors for food when they are living in a restaurant, especially in this cold weather. I showed him the cockroach traps that I was using and that were clearly not working. In fact I think the cockroaches were using them as their holiday homes. The landlord proceeded to walk around the apartment and place these bait traps in 'strategic places'. Very strategic, so much so that I hope I don't get up during the night and accidently stand on one. Apparently, I have to check the traps regularly and apply more bait when the cockroaches have eaten all the bait.

I got up during the night and went to the kitchen for some water. There perched on the ceiling was this huge cockroach. It didn't even move when I approached it. Now I'm not sure if they had already eaten the bait or whether they were just eyeing out the bait. Even though it is fake food, I was assured that the cockroaches would find it delicious. Maybe the cockroach was doing a Homer Simpson number. You know the one. He sees delicious food and then his arms fall at his side, his head tilts back, drool starts to pour out the side of his mouth and all he can muster is, "Aaaarrgghhh!" Now I'm not sure how this bait works. For

> *all I know they could eat the bait and then explode. So I was not about to kill this one. I would rather wait and see what happens. I have great expectations of this bait and have now declared war on the cockroaches. I still have to decide how I'm going to record my "kills" though. Maybe I will just carve a notch on the side of my fridge for every kill I get? I will keep you posted.*

ARRIVAL AT SCHOOL

"Hi ho, hi ho, it's off to work we go!" – Snow White and the seven dwarfs

If you are one of the lucky ones, you would have attended a few days of orientation before arriving at your school and will have a rough idea as to what to expect. For others, you would have probably arrived the day before and now starting your first day of school the following day. Alternatively, you could have arrived on a weekend, which means you would have the weekend to settle in and then only go to school on the Monday. You may have more than one co-teacher that you will teach with, but the school will assign a main co-teacher to whom you must report. This is the person who is going to look after you for the duration of your contract. They will be the link between you and the school. They will also be the ones who will assist you in getting settled in and arranging things like your Alien Registration Card, Health Card, bank account, etc. If you don't live within a few minutes walking distance from the school, it is more than likely that your new co-teacher will come and fetch you and take you to your new school on your first day. Anticipation of your first day at school can be quite scary, as you are not sure if you going to be able to cope or whether you are going to be treated well. Just remember, when schools do their recruitment drives for potential new students, they will always invariably boast that they have their own foreign English teacher at the school. So, it makes sense for your school to ensure that you feel happy and comfortable in your new environment. They generally will do all they can to assist you in making that happen anyway.

The first thing that you will notice when you arrive at the school is that you will be handed a pair of slippers and asked to remove your shoes. Don't be alarmed they are not trying to steal your shoes. It is Korean custom not to wear shoes inside temples and inside their homes. It is the same with schools. In the foyer of the school building will be small lockers in which the shoes are stored. In all likelihood, the school will assign a locker to you. When you leave the building, you remove your shoes from the locker and place the slippers back in the locker. It is advisable to wear socks at all times. The female teachers at my school wore inner socks with their shoes, so that when they wore slippers or had to remove their shoes when going into a restaurant or a person's home, their feet were still covered.

The first people that you will be introduced to are the Principal and Vice-Principal. Respect must be shown to someone older than you. Also keep in mind that they dye their hair black and look quite young, so it is very difficult to tell how old they are. When you meet someone who is older than you, you should bow first and then shake hands. You might not get to meet the rest of the staff and teachers straight away, but maybe later during the day you will be introduced to them. In most cases you will find that only your co-teacher/s can speak English and that many of the Korean teachers can't. So don't feel despondent if all you get is a handshake and a short "Hello" from them. At some point during your first week, you will attend a staff meeting or a school assembly where you will be asked to address the staff and/or students. This is an introduction of yourself and can be very brief, maybe lasting two or three minutes. Don't be too concerned about what they will think or say. Their levels of English will more than likely be very low. I remember when I gave my introductory "speech" to about fifty teachers and admin staff at my school. To this day, I can't remember what I said in my brief two minute speech, but I did receive a thunderous round of applause for my efforts. In fact, I think the applause lasted longer than my "speech". The point is that most of them didn't understand what I said, but they still wanted to make me feel welcome and hence, the thunderous applause.

During your first week you will also need to get yourself orientated and your co-teacher will be your primary source of information. It is worth mentioning that not everyone's co-teacher will be relishing the opportunity of having to look after the foreigner. If this should happen in your case, then you need to be pro-active. Don't be afraid to ask questions as they are there to support you. Find out things about your schedule, where your classroom is and the school resources that are available to you. Also ask if there are any days where you won't have to teach. There are national holidays, school festivals, sports days, field trips and examinations where you will not be required to teach. This can be useful information when doing your planning. However, be warned:

always expect the unexpected. It is not unusual for the school to make last minute changes. On numerous occasions I have spent many an hour planning for a lesson, only for it to be cancelled five minutes before it is due to take place. Your only choice in this matter is to smile and graciously accept it.

Beam Me Up, Scotty

When it came to new technology, I was always technologically challenged - now I'm just challenged. For me, uploading photos to a social media website or setting up a blog would have been an unthinkable task to accomplish. However, since coming to South Korea, I've had to "hit the ground running" and learn quite quickly. The internet connectivity here is super fast and very cheap. Believe it or not, South Korea's demand for internet connectivity would have been non-existent if it were not for computer games. Everywhere you go in town, you see these PC rooms. A PC room (not a politically correct room) is where people go to play computer games and they call them PC bangs. However, it is not just the internet technology that I now have to contend with.

At the school where I teach, they have assigned a special classroom to me from where I can teach. Well, they've always told me it was special. Although, I have often wondered why it was situated at the back-end of the school in some dingy corner! However, I digress here.

Recently, the education department gave my school a huge budget to upgrade the classroom. Hence the name change from English classroom to English lounge (expensive name change). The money was to be used to give the classroom a complete make-over and upgrade it with the latest teaching technology gadgets. I must admit that I am quite impressed with the end results. The room has been divided into various areas, with each area displaying signage above it to let the student know which area is which. The main area is used for teaching and it looks like your standard classroom layout. Another area has many books (almost like a library) with nice swivel chairs for students to sit on and is aptly named the Book Cafe. Another area is where the laptops and DVD's are kept and is known as the Computer Zone. There is also an Information Centre. Although, many students were asking me what's an "nformation Centre". I didn't know, until I realised that the "I" had fallen off the signage! The classroom has been equipped with a wonderful sound system that would make any township or informal settlement taxi driver envious. It comes with two microphones – one with a cord and the other is a cordless microphone. I get to use the cordless one and I suppose that's because I get to do most of the ducking and diving. If you have a flying desk coming at you, it's difficult to try and dodge it when you've got a mike attached to a cord! The cordless mike is great for karaoke, but when talking into the mike and trying to explain to students how to fill in a worksheet you're holding, it becomes a challenge. Rather give me one of those secret service ones, where you have the earpiece in your ear and you talk into your sleeves, "Students, this is your teacher speaking, fill in the worksheet!" It'll freak the students out – not because of the deep secret agent like voice, but because I only wear short sleeve shirts! There is also a PC with internet connectivity at the front of the classroom. This is fantastic. Furthermore, there are six laptops for the students to use. Yes, I know what you're thinking – that's a lot of solitaire! The laptops also have internet connectivity. Then there is this gadget on the teacher's desk that operates like a microscope. You put a document underneath it, and it magnifies it and projects it onto your PC and onto the flat screen TV in front of the class. One day I leaned over to get something on the desk and my arm passed under the lens of this gadget. My co-teacher almost jumped a mile high when she saw this huge hairy thing on the PC screen. She soon calmed down when I told her it was "armless" and she needn't be afraid! The classroom also has a state of the art DVD machine - even the remote control looks intimidating. I'm almost convinced it can make coffee too. I just haven't found the percolate button yet! Then there is my favourite toy, the flat screen TV. It has "touch screen" capabilities, as well as having the ability to write on the screen with your finger. They say that the pen is mightier than the sword. I wonder how the pen would compare to the finger. No more rushing back to the teachers' staffroom to try and wash the chalk off my hands. The beauty of all this sophisticated technology is that I can now operate my lessons from in front of the TV. No more having to stand at the desk bending over a PC.

I've gone from having an old dilapidated classroom, to having the "flagship" classroom of the school. All the teachers in our staff room still have to wash their hands after their lessons, as they are still using chalk and chalkboards. Now I can get my own back. After each of my lessons, I can walk in and check to see if any of the other teachers are looking at me. If they are, I can grab a tissue and begin to *wipe my fingers, smiling knowingly and saying, "Ah, the TV screen very greasy today!"*

In your first week at the school, you will probably not be required to teach a lesson. You will more than likely spend the first week introducing yourself to all of your students. One can get quite creative with this and still teach them English at the same time. I prepared a power point presentation with things about myself and my country. We then played Bingo using the information contained in the presentation. Admittedly, it does become a bit monotonous for you and your co-teacher when you have to present it to twenty one classes! It would certainly do you no harm to prepare something before leaving your home country. A few things I should advise you about when being introduced to your students for the first time. They will ask if you are married or have a girlfriend or boyfriend. If your answer is no to this question, make sure you have a suitable answer to satisfy their curiosity. They will ask you how old you are. They might even ask you your blood type. To Westerners these questions might seem impolite, but it's quite acceptable within their culture. They are just trying to get to know you a little better. Many of them would not have been exposed to Western culture. So don't be surprised if they tell you that you look like Julia Roberts or Brad Pitt. In my case it was Mel Gibson. Brave Heart was aired on one of their TV channels before I arrived in Korea. I can honestly say that I look nothing like Mel Gibson, except for the hands of course. We both have two hands! Their English vocabulary for describing someone will generally be low. So expect to be called cute, handsome or beautiful. This may not necessarily be correct, but it does wonders for the confidence.

There are also non-teaching related issues that you will have to sort out during your first week or so at your school. You will need to apply for an Alien Registration Card (ARC), Health Insurance Card, as well as having to go for a medical. It's important that you apply for your ARC as soon as possible. You cannot open a bank account or be issued a Health Insurance Card without it. You will also need it to apply for a telephone and internet, although sometimes the school may install a telephone and/or internet on your behalf. It takes about seven business days to process your ARC application and approximately one to two weeks for your Health Insurance Card. If you intend travelling outside of Korea during your vacation period, make sure to upgrade your E2 visa to a multiple entry visa when applying for your ARC. If you still have a single entry visa and leave the country, they will not allow you back in.

The school will also have a canteen where students, teachers and staff are served lunch. They will ask you if you would like to eat in the canteen or not. Some schools offer the lunch to foreign teachers for free, while others charge a minimal fee. Don't feel bad if they charge you for the meal, as your Korean colleagues also have to pay for the privilege. The school will deduct the money from your salary at the end of each month. Although the meals might not look appetizing, they are very nutritious. At every meal you will get a portion of rice and soup, as well as an assortment of side dishes like kimchi (fermented cabbage).

Hello from South Korea

It seems like just the other day I was boarding my flight for South Korea and here we are some months later. Having just run the Two Oceans Ultra marathon on the Saturday, I was expecting to hobble onto the plane on the Monday morning. However, I think my thoughts were somewhere else. Bizarre thoughts popping into my head about the mile-high club! Besides, I have been flying for more than 20 years now (no, my arms don't get tired) and it was about time. Needless to say, the pilot must have sensed my aspirations and that Singaporean so-and-so flew just under a mile high the whole way to South Korea – so much for that!

On arrival at school the following day, I had a rough idea as to what would happen. Your first port of call is to the hospital for your medical check-up. I am always hesitant because I have the potential to embarrass myself during these tests. I walked into one room (for the urine sample) and saw the nurse standing a few metres away waiting for me. She picked up a plastic cup, put it on the table and motioned me to fill it. I felt like saying, "From here? I've come here to be a teacher not a fireman and in any case my hose isn't long enough!" But I restrained myself, as last year I almost embarrassed myself. Last year the nurse gave me the plastic cup in the one hand and I held out my other hand in the anticipation that she was going to put a glossy girlie magazine and an adult DVD in it. It was my first year. How was I supposed to know it was a urine sample! I took the cup from her and said, "I won't pee long" (that one went right over her head – they are quite short you know) and then made a p-line for the toilet. Just to spite the nurse I filled the cup up to the brim and was tempted to ask for a second cup. I handed the cup to her and thought, "Yeah, let's see you walk with this and not spill any!" Word of warning: Don't try this unless you are sure they've taken blood first. To my horror, the blood was still to be taken. I'm sure I saw this evil grin on the nurse's face when she tried to jab my vein with what one can only describe as a knitting needle. I mean for goodness' sake – these people wrote on a piece of rice! Surely they have smaller needles?

The part of the job I'm looking forward to is where I have to sit down with my co-teacher and go through all the public holidays and exam days. There are so many. One interesting day she mentioned was "erections" day. I had visions of a particular day where all the men walk around with these bulges in their pants – looking something similar to the nose cone of a Boeing747. However, I quickly realised that maybe her pronunciation was a bit off or perhaps her "r" and "l's" are sometimes interchangeable. The education departments Election Day is coming up soon. Their run-up to their elections is quite festive. They don't have their candidates singing songs like "mshini wam" (ala President Zuma), but they do play upbeat music from their "campaign vehicles". You often see these vehicles parked on the side of a busy road or traffic circle. Music blaring from their speakers and these election helpers doing what one can only describe as the macarena (…when I dance they call me macarena, and the boys they say they all want me, they can't have me…hey, macarena – don't pretend you never used to dance to it now) or some other type of line dancing. They all wear their candidate's brightly coloured clothes with white gloves and then do their hand movements and dance. I'm often tempted to go and stand nearby and wave to them. Foreigners are very popular here, so I can see it would be a distraction. I can just see them going through their macarena dance routine – then I wave…aaah, she handsome foreigner (they never seem to get the sex of the person right, but always spot-on when it comes to looks). By this time you've probably got arms and elbows flaying in all different directions and total chaos amongst the "synchronised dancers".

One thing I can say about the Koreans is that their government departments work. My medical examination (blood, x-ray, etc) took about 30 minutes – including waiting time. I also had to go to the immigration office for my alien registration. I felt like walking into their offices and saying, "Hi, I'm an extra-terrestrial and I'm here to register and by the way I would like to phooone hoooome!" It took me all of 20 minutes to upgrade my visa and arrange an alien registration card...and there was no need to offer them a "monetary incentive" either!

Mind you, if I had said something like, "you scratch my back and I will scratch your back. Nudge nudge, wink wink." They would probably take my meaning literally and both parties would end up with raw backs, bruised elbows and a severe eye twitch...and I would still not have my alien registration card! They seem quite honourable. Earlier last year, there were major demonstrations in the streets because the government wanted to import American beef and they were worried about Mad Cow Disease. Due to the huge pressure created by the demonstrations, the parliament offered to resign. Where else in the world will you get a government that is willing to accept responsibility like that? Even the Korean machinery is effective. My washing machine plays this musical tune to alert you that it is finished. It's the highlight of my Sunday night...sitting by the washing machine so you can hear the tune when it finishes!

I remember when I went to one of my first classes for this year. I was mobbed by about thirty six girls. They were all around me, shouting, "Oh, you're so handsome and kind." Of course, I had to take their word for it, as they are twelve year olds and they know everything. They also said that I had "dongan". When I heard that, I thought it was something

huge. My immediate reaction was to look down and see if my fly was open. However, it's not about size...as most women will tell you...shortly after they burst into fits of laughter. No, I'm not speaking from personal experience. I have this friend of a friend, whose friend's uncle's brother met a gay biker whose boyfriend's nephew had a girlfriend and it happened to him. "Dongan" is when you are old, but you look much younger than your actual age.
So, if you come to Korea, lie about your age and you too can also have "dongan!"

Here is a typical apartment bathroom with shower, toilet and basin. Notice the little plastic bin next to the toilet? This is where you discard all your used toilet paper.

CHAPTER 4

LET'S TEACH

TEAM TEACHING

"I think Smithers picked me because of my motivational skills. Everyone says they have to work a lot harder when I'm around." - Homer Simpson

In 2010 there was a significant change to the EPIK contract, in that it stated that the Guest English Teacher (that's you and I) can be required to teach classes by themselves without a Korean teacher. Previously, it mentioned that the Guest English Teachers (GET's) shall teach classes with a Korean teacher. The implications of this are that you might be sent to a school and have to teach alone without the help of a Korean teacher. I know of teachers who are currently working in South Korea and still have Korean co-teachers teaching with them, even though the change has been made in the contract. Therefore, your school will determine whether or not you will teach with a co-teacher. It would be advisable to ask your school right from the start as to what their policy is. If you are going to be teaching with a co-teacher, you will also need to find out what their participation will be. I have had GETs tell me that that their co-teachers sometimes don't come to classes, come into the class every few minutes to check up on things and then leave, sit at the back of the class and just observe or as in my case, are involved in the lesson and help it run smoothly. Knowing what your Korean co-teacher's participation levels are will help you to plan your lessons more effectively.

The concept of team teaching is that you and your Korean co-teacher share the teaching equally i.e. fifty-fifty. However, that is an ideal situation and doesn't always work out that way. This is why it is so important to discuss your roles right at the beginning. There is an expectation that GET's will teach in a different way. So your Korean co-teacher should be quite receptive to your views on how the classes should run. I will illustrate the concept of team teaching by way of example of how we implemented it at my school. I taught grades one, two and three at a middle school. Each grade had seven classes and I was assigned four co-teachers to help me teach all twenty one classes. There was no assigned text book for my grade one classes, as this was an extra English lesson per week. I was given carte blanche as to what I wanted to teach them. This allowed me to be creative and I would link my lesson into whatever was being taught with the Korean teacher's English lesson at that time. My role was to teach the lesson topic. My co-teacher's role was to translate the new vocabulary words being taught, classroom management and assisting me with any group work that took place. However, our roles changed for our second and third grade classes. In both second and third grade classes we had an assigned text book from which to work. For the second and third grade classes, I would explain the new words being taught. The co-teacher would always check their understanding by asking them, "What did he say?" Once they had understood the meaning of the word, she would then translate it into Korean for them. The dialogue part of the text book, known as, "Let's Talk", was always done by me. I would read the dialogue and the students would repeat after me. My co-teacher would check that the students understood all the new phrases and catch words in the dialogue. Once they had grasped this, she would then translate it into Korean. We jointly monitored the class when they were doing group work. If students had any queries they would ask either of the two teachers that were available. In some cases I would maybe only teach forty percent of the class, while the co-teacher taught sixty percent. Other times I might have taught most of the class, while the co-teacher taught only a small portion. It really was dependent on the content of the lesson and what we had agreed upon at the beginning of the year.

A last point worth mentioning on team teaching is that of translation. Are you going to allow it or not? If so, to what degree are you going to allow it? There is nothing more annoying than a co-teacher who translates everything that you say without giving the students a chance to think for themselves. In my own experience I have found that when the co-teacher continually translates, some students won't even bother to listen to what I am saying. They would rather wait until I'm finished speaking and then listen to the co-teacher for the translation. That said; remember that each class will have varying levels of English ability. Lower level classes may require more translation than your other classes. Furthermore, some of the Korean co-teachers also only teach their English classes in Korean.

Big Brother is Watching You!

We have just had a five day holiday celebrating Chuseok, the Korean equivalent of Thanksgiving. So the focus of my teaching this past week has been Chuseok and getting the students to be able to express and communicate part of their culture in English. This week's classes also included the dreaded "observation lesson." I know this might conjure up images of a foreign English teacher being subjected to having electrodes and wires attached to them, whilst Korean men and women dressed in little white coats, poke and prod the unsuspecting foreigner. However, this couldn't be further from the truth. An observation lesson is where a group, swarm, herd or gaggle (not sure of the collective form) of teachers and administrative staff observe the English foreign teacher and their Korean co-teacher doing team teaching in their lesson.

So, let me start by giving you a little more background information on this observation lesson. I was a bit wary as to why they called it an observation lesson and wanted to know the importance of it. My co-teacher mentioned that it was to evaluate how I was performing, as a teacher that is, and that they could use this evaluation to decide whether or not to offer me a contract renewal. That's what she said. All I heard in my mind was, "You don't have the right to remain silent. Anything you say can and will be used against you in a court of law..." After much deliberation, we decided that the theme for our lesson would be Chuseok. Together my co-teacher and I only spent about an hour or so discussing the actual lesson and its contents. She spent more than a week compiling a thirty page document for the observation lesson, on amongst other things, why English is important and how students feel about learning English. My documentation was a one page lesson plan that consisted of the flow of the lesson and the four skills to be covered.

The dreaded day had arrived. My classroom was packed with students and "observers". The "observation team" sat at the back of the classroom and a large proportion of them couldn't even speak or understand English. I'm bound to score highly on English ability. Perched in the corner, behind the observation team, was the video camera to record the lesson. I wasn't sure if that was for prosperity or evidence? I just hope they capture my good side. Come to think of it, I don't think I have a good side.

Lights! Camera! Action! We started the lesson with our normal greeting or "Insa" as they call it. I proceeded to ask my co-teacher what she did over Chuseok. She would then go into a power point presentation on her activities over the Chuseok weekend. I would then ask further questions about the contents of the presentation. After having done about fifteen lessons on Chuseok one tends to want to say, "Yeah, yeah...talk to the hand" to all the replies. Although in the presentation, I must admit that she was wearing a beautiful traditional dress which is called a Hanbok. The dress that is, not my co-teacher. I then took the microphone and began to meander among the students and asked them about their Chuseok weekend. I started to have thoughts about the Jerry Springer show. What if I asked one of these kids to tell me what they did over the Chuseok weekend and they start to divulge stuff that would make a sailor blush. We then asked the students to give us describing words for various activities that took place during the Chuseok weekend. Once *all of these words were up on the board, we then divided the students into groups and assigned a specific Chuseok activity to them. They were to discuss amongst their group members their specific topic and then do a presentation to the rest of the class on what they had come up with. I was pleasantly surprised with the results. They all seemed to fare very well at being able to express and communicate their culture in English.*

What about that observation team? Our principal was coerced into being there and after about ten minutes, started browsing the books and DVDs in the classroom. Then while no-one was looking, promptly snuck out of the room. I'm not sure if this was in absolute disgust at the selection of books and DVDs in the classroom or our lesson! At least he could've waited until I turned my back. Come to think of it, many Koreans are afraid to speak English to a foreigner and the mere thought of having to, sends them scurrying. The observation criteria were mainly about the documentation and how relevant it was, and very little about the foreign teacher's performance. I asked my co-teacher if that were the case, why we had to do the observation lesson in the first place. She responded by saying that according to my contract I am required to do an observation lesson once a year. Remember when you were young and your mother asked you to do something and you replied, "Why?" She would then respond by saying, "Because I said so!" At that moment I kind of had that feeling. My wearing a tie, smart shirt and pants for the occasion, seemed to have been wasted on the moment. Although, some students did mention that I looked handsome. Kids, you've got to love 'em!

So how did we do in the observation lesson? The lesson ran smoothly and the feedback was positive. So it seems that we live to teach another day.

CLASSROOM MANAGEMENT

"Go ahead, punk. Make my day." – Harry Callahan

I wouldn't use this line on your students, unless of course you are Harry Callahan (Clint Eastwood) from the 1971 movie, Dirty Harry. Each school and each teacher will have their own views and methods on how to control their classes. Therefore, it is advisable that you decide how you want to implement classroom management. Give some thought to what you would like and then make a decision on what your expectations are. What is acceptable behaviour in the classroom? How will I maintain and enforce discipline? What are the rules for the classroom? Etc.

Bear in mind that the behaviour of Korean students can differ from Western classroom behaviour. Students may not make eye contact with you when addressing you. This should not be seen as being impolite, but rather a sign of respect. Some might be the noisiest in your class, but when asked a question, they reply in a very low tone of voice. This again is a sign of respect and should not be construed as someone with little or no confidence. Students are also afraid of making mistakes and being ridiculed in front of others and will therefore be hesitant to volunteer.

Once you have an idea of what your expectations are, discuss it with your co-teacher. Don't be set in your ways and inflexible. If your co-teacher makes some changes and suggestions, be flexible enough to cater for those changes. They have been teaching Korean students longer than you and would have a wealth of experience of which you can tap into.

I think take the advice of many an educator when they say that you should be firm, fair and consistent. Students will quickly assess the situation in your class and realise what they will be allowed to get away with. If you initially go into the classroom wanting to be everyone's friend and the chaos does erupt, it is going to be difficult to regain control as they won't respect your authority. However, if you go in being firm from day one, it's easier to ease off a little later on, as you have already established your control and authority in the classroom. I was very fortunate, after discussing classroom management with my co-teachers, it was agreed that they would take care of the discipline and I would take care of the rest. That meant I could go around 'high-fiving' my students whenever they got something right, but as soon as chaos erupted, I would just turn to my co-teachers and rely on them to install calm.

Hell Hath No Fury Like a Woman Scorned

The 11th of November is a special day in South Korea. It is known as Pepero Day and I suppose one could say that it has some similarities to Valentine's Day. On this day friends and lovers give each other Pepero and other chocolates. Pepero are pretzel sticks dipped in chocolate. The 1s in eleventh (11) of November (11) are said to represent the Pepero sticks. Being a teacher on Pepero Day has its advantages. Teachers often get given boxes of Pepero or small chocolates from their students. I was lucky to have been given some by my students, but unlucky for the potential weight that I am going to gain from eating too many Peperos. Besides the potential weight gain, the other downside is that students are bound to be hyped up after that entire sugar intake.

The third period of the day I had to teach English to my second grade students. Their English ability is very low and my co-teacher and I struggle to get them to listen to us at the best of times. So today would be no different, except of course that they would be high on sugar from all the chocolates and Pepero sticks!

The lesson started off with me explaining the new vocabulary and then moving on to the target dialogue. The target dialogue is a basic dialogue between two people, normally Sujin and Minho! Yes, I'm afraid to say it, but those good old days when we used to read about Janet and John are over. It's all Sujin, Minho and Inho now, real British and American names. Where was I? Oh, yes. The target dialogue will also contain an English expression that we want to teach them i.e. asking for advice or directions, etc. We then do a pattern drill where I will read the dialogue and they will repeat after me. I then take the role of one person in the dialogue and the class takes the other part and we role-play the dialogue. After that, we then change roles and role-play again. Finally, the students get to practice and role-play the dialogue amongst themselves. I will then take volunteers and two students will stand up and role-play the dialogue in front of the class. On most occasions they get the dialogue right and they are rewarded with more candy! So those sugar levels are continually climbing.

Somewhere through our second set of target dialogue, my co-teacher lost it. Some of the students were talking amongst themselves and not listening, when they were supposed to be repeating the dialogue after me. You know when the Korean co-teachers are angry because they always start off with the same thing. They shout, "Children" (but in Korean) and then followed by a string of dialogue that sounds like rapid machine gun fire to the untrained ear. For all I know, she could have threatened them within an inch of their young lives, because all of a sudden they were absolutely quiet. Not that I was complaining. My co-teacher turned to me and said, "Sorry, punishment. I'm angry." I have been doing this teaching thing now for almost two years, but nothing could have prepared me for what was about to take place.

I have thirty six students in this class and these small desks are in clusters of six and placed in the shape of a T. My co-teacher made all the students get onto their desks. They then had to kneel on the desks and then sit down on their feet, without their knees leaving the table top. Under normal circumstances, if you did this by yourself it is relatively easy to do. However, there are six of you in this small confined space all trying to do the same thing at once. It was quite humorous to watch. Once they had managed to simultaneously achieve some semblance of balance, one would end up losing their balance. This would cause a ripple effect and everyone else would lose their balance. There was this constant shaking noise of desks, albeit from different directions in the room. If I had known this was going to happen, I would have brought my baton along to conduct my class of shaking desks!

However, it seems that the students weren't the only ones that were experiencing a sugar rush from all the Peperos and chocolates that day. I run an English workshop for English teachers every Wednesday from 2pm to 5pm. It was during this workshop that one of the Korean teachers came bursting into the room with a panicked look in his eye and started rattling something off in Korean. Judging by the look on the other Koreans faces and by the urgency of the messenger, I expected the worst. For a moment I thought maybe North Korea had invaded South Korea. The two teachers made a hasty exit to go and resolve the urgent crisis. It turns out that the only fighting that took place was between two students and one ended up with a bloodied lip. No need for all the hype. Too much sugar in the blood for all concerned if you ask me!

Having a co-teacher to assist you with classroom management is all fair and well. However, did I mention that you will also be required to teach after school hours without a co-teacher? As mentioned in an earlier chapter, you might be required to do summer and winter camps. I also mention later on in this chapter that you will be required to do the afterschool programme or English Club as some schools prefer to call it. In both these instances, it is highly unlikely that you will have a co-teacher to assist you. This means that you will be responsible for the students in your class. This is why it is important for you to adhere to the initial advice offered about being consistent, firm and fair. Remember students would have already realised what they can get away with from your regular class hours. I want to impress upon you that under no circumstances are you to use any form of physical discipline in the classroom. You could find yourself in serious trouble with your school, the students' parents and not to mention the Department of Education. Corporal punishment has also been banned and in metropolitan cities like Seoul, there is a further ban on "physical" types of punishments such as sit-ups and push-ups. Just because it is banned, does not mean that it does not occur. You may still see some Korean teachers making use of some types of physical punishments. There is no need to resort to the use of physical punishment. A quick internet search will reveal a host of reward and punishment strategies that one can employ. I used non-verbal discipline to great effect. If a student was rowdy or causing a distraction in the class, I would slowly walk towards them and hang around in their vicinity. They would realise that I had noticed them and that I was not happy with their behaviour. Another technique would be to walk past them and give them a gentle touch on their shoulder, implying, "I've spotted you making a noise. Now be quiet." Glaring at the noisy student/s; pointing at them and then raising your finger to your lips to imply silence; wait until the class falls silent before continuing, or if all else fails, stomping your foot on the ground. One of the things that I discovered with some of the classes is that for some reason, the boys and girls did not like to sit next to each other. This played into my hands, because when they continued to misbehave I would move the students into different seats. I would ensure that the seating arrangement went boy, girl, boy, girl, etc. They could no longer chat with their friends and they became quiet because they were now sitting next to someone of the opposite sex. If you still struggle with discipline, you could employ some of the disciplining methods that the Korean teachers use i.e. getting the students to stand at the back of the classroom facing the wall.

LESSON PLANNING

"Failing to plan is planning to fail."- Proverb

At the beginning of my first semester in South Korea, lesson planning was by far the most stressful thing for me to do. I had majored in marketing and sales management and not teaching. To add to this stress was the fact that it was difficult to gauge the level of the students' abilities, as each class was different. Also keep in mind that I had twenty one classes to teach. I think it was after my second week of teaching that I decided to go into Seoul on the weekend and buy some books from the Kyobo bookstore. Needless to say, these books didn't prove to be too useful either. Don't get me wrong. My lessons weren't a total disaster. Sometimes they would be aimed at the low level students, then students with a higher level of English ability would get bored and vice versa. I have even had seasoned professional teachers come to me with similar types of problems. It took me several months of trial and error before I finally got the balance right. The reason I mention all of this is in case you find yourself in a similar situation. Don't panic or worry and above all don't be too hard on yourself. As the old adage goes, "This too shall pass." Just keep plugging away at it and eventually everything will fall into place.

Now that I have vanquished that fear, let me install another one. In your first month of teaching your co-teacher may ask you to prepare a semester plan for the entire semester. A semester plan is an overview of what you are going to teach for the semester. I remember my co-teacher asked me and she said she wanted the semester plan by the following day. I wish I could say that I had sleepless nights about it, but I can't because I really only had one night to be sleepless. This sounds quite a daunting task but it's not really. When I was told that I had to do one, I did express my concerns with my co-teacher. I mentioned that I still needed to assess the students' English levels and couldn't possibly commit to lessons based on the fact that I didn't know what level to pitch it at. She suggested that I just write down the topics of the lesson and a description of what I would cover e.g. fours skills, grammar, etc. They would not hold me to exactly what I was going to teach on what day. I could make changes as I went along. The semester plan is just for bureaucratic reasons. If the supervisor from the local office of education office comes to visit, they have something to show them. I know that when I handed my semester plan to my co-teacher, she hardly looked at it. It was photocopied and handed to the administration office. Hopefully that's another of your fears that I've sent packing.

When doing your lesson planning it's a good idea to keep a schedule of which lessons are being taught to which grades and classes on a weekly basis. You will find that classes can be rescheduled or cancelled at short notice. I have had classes cancelled because students had exams, tests, class photos had to be taken, flu inoculations had to be given to the students, as well as things like field trips and sports days. Not to mention classes that are rescheduled because another teacher needs your time slot, as they have to go on a business trip somewhere. It becomes quite difficult to remember which class did which lesson and during which week it was taught. I had a very simple weekly schedule that I created to help me track what was being taught and to whom. I took my lesson roster which contained the days of the week and the classes that I would teach for that week. I then created a spreadsheet in MS Excel and put the lesson roster data into the spreadsheet. One spreadsheet page equalled one week and I created a spreadsheet page for each week. Whatever happened on that day for that class was logged onto the spreadsheet. If the lesson was to be carried over to the following lesson, this could be noted on the spreadsheet. This gave me a quick overview as to which lessons had been taught and to whom and when.

Example:

Week: 1 Nov – 5 Nov

	1	2	3	4	5
Mon	Grade 1-6 Weather	Grade 2-3 Cancelled	Grade 2-6 Let's Talk		Grade 1-1 Weather
Tues		Grade 2-4 Let's Talk		Grade 1-5 Weather	Grade 2-2 Let's Talk
Wed	Grade 1-2 Weather	Grade 3-3 Advice	Grade 3-6 Cancelled	Grade 1-7 Cancelled	
Thurs	Grade 1-4 Weather		Grade 3-4 Advice		Grade 3-1 Advice
Fri		Grade 3-5 Advice	Grade 1-3 Weather	Grade 3-2 Advice	Grade 3-7 Advice

The above example is just an illustration of how to implement a weekly schedule. Under normal circumstances you would be allocated twenty two hours per week over seven periods per day and not five. You will note that Grade 1-7, Grade 2-3 and Grade 3-6 had their lessons cancelled. This would mean that they would have to do the Weather (1-7), Let's Talk (2-3) and Advice (3-6) lessons the following week, whilst the other grades continued with a new lesson.

Now to the part that caused me much stress in the first few months of teaching, actual lessons to teach the students. Your school may have prescribed text books from which you can teach. This would mean that you will not have to create your own lessons as you can utilise the text books. For those who don't have prescribed textbooks, you will unfortunately have to do a lot more work than those who do have. Whether you do or don't have a prescribed textbook, you will still need to plan for the after school program, as well as the winter and summer camps. It is very seldom that foreign teachers are given textbooks with which to teach these programmes. So how does one come up with ideas for lessons? One needs to look at your semester schedule and check if anything is happening on specific dates. For instance, there might be a school sports day or traditional holiday coming up. A great topic for a lesson could be sports or you could include something from your own culture like Halloween. I was fortunate to be teaching around the time of the Olympics and the soccer world cup, so I could include both those as topics for my lessons. If you run out of ideas, go with tried and tested topics like shopping, transport, sport, pets, hobbies, restaurant, directions, travel, money, holidays, etc. It is very easy to create a scenario around these topics where you can teach new vocabulary, grammar and the four skills (reading, writing, listening and speaking). One could also have one topic, but stretch it over two lessons. I did a lesson on fashion. In the first lesson I taught them fashion vocabulary and how to describe what a person was wearing. In the second lesson I had them create an outfit for a person using cut-outs from magazines. They would then describe the outfit and present it to the class. When planning a lesson always have a backup plan. It's good to have a few extra fun activities that you could use just in case the lesson finishes early. Another good practice is to have an extra lesson plan prepared. There might be an occasion where you are asked to teach an extra class that was not on your schedule and that extra lesson will come in handy.

Life's Little Lessons

The school officially closes on the 29th December. However, it's as good as over. My students start writing exams this week. Once the exams are finished, there are only two weeks of school left. No point in teaching them anything new, as they would have already finished the syllabus. So it looks like movies and games for the two weeks of lessons leading up to the end of the semester.

The school year has flown by and I really don't know where the time has gone. Teaching nine hundred students, week after week, might seem like it gets a little monotonous, but I really have had some good times. If I would have to choose which my favourite grade to teach is, I would have to say my first graders. These are your twelve to fourteen year olds. I'm given carte blanche when it comes to designing the lesson plans for first graders and don't have a set curriculum to follow. Sometimes it can be a nightmare to generate new ways and ideas to teach them English, but it's worth the stress when you see the results the students come up with. The first graders are straight out of elementary school and aren't afraid to express their creativity. When it comes to some second and third graders, they seem to feel that it's beneath them to get too excited about being creative in English.

I started thinking back to some of the lessons that I had done over the last few months. Some of them were quite memorable; some had their moments, while others were quite a nightmare to manage. I remember one of the first 'creative' lessons I tried. It was near the beginning of the semester and I wanted to teach students expressions around rules i.e. things you can do, things you can't do and things you are allowed to do. So I gave them a few examples about rules of the road, at the library and in a restaurant. I then split them up into groups and asked them to draw up some rules for the classroom. They seem to have grasped the idea. We had rules about not fighting in class, keeping quiet while the teacher was talking and paying attention, etc. Then there were even some odd ones like no drinking alcohol or smoking in class. Bloody hell! I should hope not, especially if you are not going to share with the teacher.

Spurred on by the success of the 'rules' lesson, I decided to try and get them to write a story in English. It involved a few pages of clipart. The students were put into groups and had to choose six pictures from the clipart. They then had to place the clipart in a sequence and write a story about it. The majority of the students wrote stories about marriage, divorce and extra-marital affairs. One wonders where these kids come up with their ideas. Never under estimate the power of television and Korean soap operas.

One of my favourite lessons was the one about fashion. I taught the students new vocabulary relating to fashion accessories, clothing and how to describe what a person was wearing. I then split them up into groups and gave them a pile of magazines. They had to cut out pictures of clothing and accessories, stick them onto a cut-out person and then describe what the person was wearing. The girls took to this lesson and came up with some really creative designs. So what about the boys? Well, boys will be boys. They were cutting out all the pictures of panties and bras and making their near naked models. After each lesson I would always put some of the students work up on the board at the back of the classroom. I couldn't help notice that some of the boys were always going to this one picture and lifting up the dress and looking under it. My co-teacher must have also noticed and eventually glued it down. Now I'm not sure what the students had put under there for them to be so curious, but I wasn't about to go and look for myself. Can you imagine if I did go take a look and someone just happened to walk in or notice me doing it? How do you try and explain to them that you were just looking to see what the students were up to, without them suspecting you of being a pervert!

A more recent lesson I did, was one about Halloween. I gave them a picture of the various parts of a skeleton. They had to cut out the parts and then assemble the skeleton and paste it onto a sheet of paper. The students would name the skeleton and then tell a little story about it. The boys seemed to have fared a bit better than the girls this time around. However, this didn't stop some of them getting up to mischief. One of the groups had taken one of the leg bones *of the skeleton and placed it in the centre of the skeleton's body to represent a male sex organ. They could not contain their excitement to show me their handy work. "Look teacher. Scary Skeleton has a big penis!" My co-teacher was well aware of this group's endeavour, but still chose them to present their artwork to the whole class. She still came to me afterwards to say how embarrassed she was by their presentation. Hello? Then why did you choose them to present?*

Even though there have been ups and downs throughout the year, on the whole I think it has been a good year of teaching. I will always have fond memories of teaching my first graders. Let's see what the new semester brings.

I followed a set daily routine for all my classes. This made the lessons flow easily and allowed the students to feel more comfortable as they knew what to expect. Firstly, it is a good idea to put your students into groups right at the start of the semester. When you have a lesson that involves group work, you can just instruct the students to get into their assigned groups. This way there is less disruption in the class and you do not waste valuable time having to assign students to groups or teams. Group leaders can be chosen as and when a task is given to them. This way every student will get a chance to present the group's work. The format of the lesson rarely changed. The class would always start with the greeting. I would then tell the students what the topic for the lesson was going to be. This would be written on the board. It is a good idea to write the date on the board as well. This gives the students an opportunity to learn how to write dates in English. Once this has been done, I will inform the students about what we are going to learn that day. From here I will teach them the new vocabulary which is related to the topic and contains a maximum of ten new words. Immediately after this, we will go into the rest of the lesson which covers reading, writing, listening and speaking. Obviously, the four skills are all linked to the topic that is being covered in that lesson. I will also leave about five to ten minutes at the end of each lesson to do a fun activity. This could be in the form of a word search, crossword puzzle, or game, etc. Once the fun activity has been done, I will wrap-up the lesson by doing a quick summary of the main learning points and then saying goodbye to the students.

Your school or English department will all have their own policy and or ideas on lesson plans. Some might require you to do formal lesson plans, while others may just require you to have a rough guide as to what you are going to do. It's best to find out what their policy is and stick to that. Formal lesson plans would be ones that are typed up in a certain format and handed in and filed with your co-teacher. I was not required to do formal lesson plans, but I always had a one page document that showed me the sequence of events of the lesson and how much time to spend on each activity. If you get stuck with lesson plans, there is a plethora of websites on the internet that deal with lessons and lesson planning. One such site that I used, called "Becoming a Better EFL teacher", lists some twenty one sites that help with lesson plans and lesson planning. The exact link for that website is: http://betiereflteacher.blogspot.com/2009/09/21-places-to-find-free-esl-lesson-plans.html

You can also try the following:

http://www.eslcafe.com
http://www.enchantedlearning.com

The Games People Play

It was the start of another lesson with my favourite class, the first graders. At the start of each class, I always tell the students what we are going to be doing for the lesson. I mentioned that we would be learning some new words and that I would be splitting them up into groups so that they could plan a make-believe surprise party for one of their friends. After each group had planned their party, one member of the group would then present their party plan to the rest of the class.

It's at this point when all hell broke loose. Students started chanting, "Gawi Bawi Bo," whilst flaying their arms at each other. Some students where waving a flat hand at other students. I thought, "Geez, that student is going to give someone a snot-klap." Now 'snot-klap' is an Afrikaans word and there is no English equivalent. To give you an idea of how hard it is, imagine someone slapping you in your face with such ferocity, that mucus (snot) shoots out of your nose. Now that's being hit hard! Others looked like they were trying to protect themselves by making a peace sign (v-shape) with their hand. I assumed that was to try and poke the attacking student's eyes out. Others were just brandishing their fists about. All the while this was happening there was the continuous chanting of "Gawi Bawi Bo." All this chanting and arm movement made me think that maybe this was some kind of ancient and sacred Korean martial arts.

I come from SA, so I have been exposed to quite a bit of violence. However, I was now starting to panic. My mind was racing, "Did I switch the iron off at home? Did I leave the bath taps running? I don't even have a bath." My co-teacher must have sensed that I was unaccustomed to this behaviour and assured me that there was nothing to be alarmed about. She explained that they were in the process of deciding who in the group was going to present their party ideas to the class. The penny dropped. Gawi Bawi Bo was the equivalent of our Rock Paper Scissors.

It seemed like a very straightforward process with all students accepting the outcome first time around. Now if it was Westerners I am sure it would be a different story. No doubt there would be more than a few who would present their hand, which would be half curled, with two fingers almost forming a V, so that they can decide to change their 'sign' the moment that they have seen their opponents hand.

I was rather impressed with the process and apparently, they do this at other times whenever they need to make decisions amongst themselves. Imagine if we could use Rock Paper Scissors for all our major decisions in the world. How to resolve the Middle East conflict? "Rock, paper, scissors" Okay, we won't make any more claims on whose land this is. Should Mr Mugabe step down from power in Zimbabwe? "Rock, paper, scissors" Enjoy your retirement, Mr Mugabe. It will probably be the only time that a free and fair decision was reached in Zimbabwe.

DUTIES AND RESPONSIBILITES

"Marge, don't discourage the boy! Weaselling out of things is important to learn. It's what separates us from the animals! Except the weasel." - Homer Simpson

There will also be some duties and responsibilities that you might be required to do that are not covered in the contract. These duties and responsibilities are varied and will be dependent on what your school or English department asks of you. There are things like debating and essay writing competitions. In the town where I stayed, there was an annual debating and essay writing competition. They would hold a competition at our school and then choose the best students. These students would then go on to compete against other schools in the area. The winners would then go on to compete in the regional finals. It is quite prestigious for the individuals and the school to do well in these competitions. They may well ask you to judge in the school competition, as well as preparing the students for the local and regional competitions.

Would You Like a Fifty-Fifty Split or to Call a Friend?

Near the end of each semester the Provincial Office of Education holds an English-Up competition for all the schools within the province. An English-Up competition is a speaking competition. Students are asked a few questions about various topics and they have to answer them. They are evaluated according to accuracy, content, logicality and pronunciation. The winners of the competition then represent the province on a national level i.e. they compete against other provinces. I was asked to help coach and prepare the students for the competition. Some of the topics are quite difficult, especially if English is not your first language. I would ask the students questions, let them answer, and then give them my answer and what I thought of their answers. This would enable them to get many different points of view. One particular topic which caught my interest was about a historical person. The question I had to ask the students was, "If you could travel back in history, who would you like to meet and why?" I started to ask the first student this question and before I could finish, she shouted, "Jesus Christ!" I was quite shocked. I told her there was no need to be blasphemous and if the question was that difficult I could ask another easier question. When I saw the confused look on her face, I realised that I had misinterpreted what she had said and that was in fact whom she would like to meet.

People always ask you what is your favourite movie, singer, song or book of all time, but rarely a question about who you would like to meet if you could go back in history. When the time came for me to give my answer, I blurted out, "King Arthur." I'm not quite sure why I said King Arthur. Maybe it's just that secretly I might have fancied myself as a knight. Who knows? However, I don't think being a knight would have worked for me. I would hardly have had much time to do any knightly deeds. I would be too busy answering ads in the personal columns. "Hot supermodel seeks her knight in shining armour."

I was also tasked with judging the essay writing competition for our school. The old adage is true, "Sometimes you wonder who the teacher is and who the student." Their innocence and insights are quite remarkable, not to mention cute. The insights that these kids came up with could easily have been included in a movie like 'The Secret.' The topic for the essay competition was, "The Happiest Moment in My Life." What follows are unedited excerpts from some of the essays. "I think the happiest moment is we make it we change mind or think if you don't the happiest moment you should consider about it. But you don't have the happiest moment: you make it right now! The most important thing is you think carefully and you punish of your bad think and decide you can be the happiest person!" Well, if that's not telling you about the power of the mind, then I don't know.

Then there was this one about compassion. "One day, my friend walk the street suddenly, the begger begged to her but she had a only one dollar but she gives to him I ask her "What is the happiest moment in your life" and she said this tale!!"

Of course then you also get the ones that can be misconstrued. "I lived with Mr Lee's family. Mr Lee buy icecream for us when we masage him. Ice cream was very tastey" Bloody hell! I'm a Westerner and I'm going to think the worst. Massage him for ice cream! What were you thinking? Don't you know ice cream can cause tooth cavities!

A point worth mentioning here is that it is quite acceptable in Korea for a child to massage an adult. Even if this adult is not their parent or relative. The children are very respectful and once they have been introduced to someone, they are no longer considered a stranger. They know that adults endure stress in their lives and if asked, will massage a person in order to help that person.

> *All things considered, there were some really well written ones which stood head and shoulders above the rest. Thankfully, this made my job a lot easier.*

Your local office of education may also require you to hold English teacher workshops for the Korean English teachers in your area or school. You're probably thinking the same thing that I thought. What can I teach teachers who already hold degrees in English teaching? The thing is it's not your job to teach them anything about teaching. They want to practise and perfect their English in a safe environment. I had to run a three hour workshop for the English teachers, once a week, for ten weeks. The first thing that I did with them was to give them a questionnaire to fill out. I asked them to rate their English abilities, what areas they felt weakest in, which of the four skills they wanted to focus on, types of topics they wanted to cover, etc. This enabled me to establish what their needs were and then to plan my workshops accordingly. They seemed to love idioms and tongue twisters and I always included those in the lessons. English humour and subtleties can be quite difficult for some of the Korean teachers to pick up. I had a whole three hour lesson on the subject and it worked well. The only word of caution that I can give is to stay away from topics that are quite heavy or controversial, or at least until you know them a little better. If that's something you want to pursue in your workshops, then it would be best to ask them right in the beginning when you do your needs analysis.

Idiotic Expressions

I teach English at a middle school in South Korea. Some of you might be asking what is a middle school (a school which is between primary and high school), while others might be asking where South Korea is. I extend my deepest sympathies to the latter people. In my teachers' workshop that I run for teachers, my teachers are always interested and fascinated with English idiomatic expressions, and probably for good reason. Ever notice how close the word "idiomatic" and "idiotic" sound. Maybe it's intentional.

Take for example the idiomatic expression, "The pen is mightier than the sword." Now picture two people duelling, one with a sword and the other with a pen. The scene or conversation could go something like this:

Man with cheap pen: "Hah, I've just drawn on your hand."

Man with sword, as he lunges forward to poke his opponent's eye out: "Take that."

Man with cheap pen, as he drops the pen and clutches his eye: "What did you do that for?"

Man with sword: "Because you're a stupid git, thinking you could take me on with a pen and a cheap one at that. Haven't you heard of a Waterman pen?"

How idiotic is that? You might be saying that it is more powerful to write with a pen, but then again who writes with a sword. For goodness' sake, just compare writing instrument with writing instrument.

One that really seems idiotic to me is the one that says, "It's like shooting fish in a barrel." This expression implies that something is easy. Now why would someone want to go and do this and besides it's dangerous. You're encouraging people to act irresponsibly. If you have a couple of people standing around a barrel and you get your angle wrong, it's going to go straight through the barrel and take out one of the people. Or worse still, ricochet off the bottom of the barrel and take you out. If it's so damn easy, scoop them out – they aren't going anywhere. Better still, make it a fun activity and bring all your friends around and you can "dunk" for them.

Then there is the one about, "If you lie down with dogs, you get up with fleas." Now this is just plain nonsense. During the Korean War food was quite scarce. Due to the food shortage, Koreans used to eat dogs as an alternative food source. To imply to Koreans that one sleeps with dogs, is basically telling them it's okay to play with one's food. This would go against what most Korean and Western mothers tell their kids at the supper table; "Don't play with your food." Furthermore, I have heard one or two Koreans say, "Delicious," when a dog walks by. So now, you have this poor little animal running around thinking it has got a name (Delicious) and his owner wants to sleep with him, implying some sort of affection. Next thing the dog ends up in the pot – it's cruel to get their hopes up like that.

You might be reading this and saying, "But you're missing the point, they are not meant to be taken literally." Well then, I suggest you come and teach in South Korea and let's see how you fare. Everything is taken literally. A few tips if you are coming to teach. The first thing you might want to do is know how to clearly explain when something is to be *taken literally and when it is to be taken figuratively. Secondly, if you're hungry and you want something to eat, don't ask for a hotdog.*

You might also have to teach Korean teachers who would like to learn English. When I arrived at my school, I had a group of teachers that approached me and asked if I would teach them conversational English. I would meet with them once a week after school. The lessons lasted about ninety minutes. We kept the lessons fun and light and would talk about topics that interested them. I did not get paid for these lessons, but after each lesson the teachers would show me around town or take me to dinner. It was a great way to learn about their culture and at the same time they were getting more of an opportunity to practise their English. Don't be too concerned if your teachers decide to stop lessons for a while. Sometimes they do get too busy with other school activities and are unable to make the classes. Their motivation for learning will be high and they will return.

There will also be many teachers' meetings. Your school may or may not invite you to their weekly staff meetings. I attended the first few meetings. However, the meetings were all in Korean. I was given permission not to attend as I could not understand and they felt my time could be better utilised. There are also other meetings that take place that are work related, but are more of a fun nature. One such meeting is their field trips that the students and teachers go on. Usually it consists of anything from a day to a few days away from school. These meetings are of a voluntary nature, but I strongly urge that you take part in them. It's a wonderful opportunity to bond with your co-teacher and co-workers who do not speak English, as well as your students. The added bonus is that you won't have to teach while you're on these field trips.

> ### The Journey of a Thousand Miles
>
> *I was informed by my co-teacher that I would be accompanying the second graders on a picnic – for three days! The dictionary definition of picnic is, "an excursion or outing which the participants carry food with them and share a meal in the open air." Three days is a long time for a picnic by anybody's standards!*
>
> *So I was going on a field trip with two hundred and fifty two students. We would be travelling in buses and would have to endure a four hour drive before we reached our destination on the North East side of South Korea. I got the run down on the impending 'doom and gloom' from one of my colleagues. Bus accidents, students beating up teachers and students sneaking into teachers rooms and drawing on their faces, etc., etc. That didn't phase me. My only concern was that I had a room, any room, as long as it had a shower and a toilet that you could flush.*
>
> *There were seven buses lined up outside the school on Monday morning. One white one, the lead bus, and six red ones. Each class was assigned to a bus. Grade 2-1 in the lead bus and then, in numerical order, Grade 2-7 in the last bus. The bus drivers had to ensure that the buses stayed in this order at all times. I was quite impressed with our bus. We had a flat screen TV, a karaoke system and more importantly, a hot/cold water dispenser – ideal for my Mocha gold coffee mix sachets that I brought along. Fortunately, I never had to worry about relaxing or wondering how I was going to pass the time. I had my co-teacher sitting next to me who would tell me 'interesting' tit-bits of information every few minutes, just before I was about to nod off to sleep. Like*

the time we were travelling on a 7km bridge over the sea that the Korean's built. I was informed that it was the longest in Asia. Apparently, they asked the British to build it, but they said it couldn't be done. I'm sure they had good reason for saying that. Bloody hell! Did the bridge just sway violently in the wind or was that the bus driver swerving?

After the first two hours, the bus driver was kind enough to put on a Korean horror movie for us. Even though it was in Korean, I could get the gist of the story. I was really getting into it, when my co-teacher asked me if I wanted to know how it ends. Before I could say, "No, not unless you want a hot poker pushed up your rear-end," she told me how the whole thing ended. I suppose that did give me a chance to have a much needed cup of Mocha gold coffee.

Fortunately, we did not have to sit on the bus for four straight hours. Our itinerary included some historical sites along the way. We saw Cheongryeongpo, which was the exile place of young King Danjong. It is surrounded by a river on the North, South and East side. On the West side, it has a steep cliff and the only way you can access the place is by boat. There were other places that I would like to have seen, but we did not have time. One such place was Donggang River. The brochure had this to say about it, "Unlike other tourist resorts in Korea, it has lack of tourist facilities or information board but that's why Donggang River keeps more beautiful views." Enough said, where do I find this place.

When we arrived in the town that we were going to use as our base, I noticed this huge "statue" at the entrance to the town. At first I thought it was an outdoor advert for Adult World. However, it turns out that it is the town's mascot and they have smaller ones all over the town.

We arrived at our hotel at about 6pm. The place was called Mamoth Resortel. Now you might think that is an unusual name for a hotel. However, I'm sure Mammoth's were around when this hotel was built. I was fortunate enough to be given my own room. When I entered the room for the first time, my reaction was to call room service and tell them that my bed had been stolen.

I initially mentioned that all I wanted was a shower and a flushable toilet. Well, it looked like my wish had come true, as that's basically all I got. There was no bed or cupboards. All I had in my room was a TV, which broadcast snow with the occasional hint of a picture, and a bar fridge in the one corner. In the other corner, I had a pile of blankets and a few pillows. I had my 'shower and flushable' toilet, so I was happy. I no longer worry about what I'm going to catch from a hotel room. I just hope there's a cure!

When I went to breakfast the next morning a colleague asked me how I slept. I was tempted to say, "With one eye open," but politely answered that I had slept well – which was the truth believe it or not. There is nothing like a Korean breakfast to get you started in the morning. Rice, seaweed, soup and an unusual surprise of 'scrambled egg'. We were going to need all the sustenance we could get, as we were about to embark on a five day sight-seeing trip that was going to be fitted into three days. Fortunately, we had an experienced bus driver who would be able to get us around quickly and safely. I could see that our bus driver had certainly undertaken extensive advanced driver courses. On one occasion, we were going down a mountain pass that made Lombard Street (crookedest street in the world) in San Fransisco look straight. The bus driver was trying to change the DVD and answer his cellphone at the same time. To give him credit, he took everything in his stride. I'm not sure why some of the students had this pale shocked look on their faces, as it was a music DVD playing and not a horror movie.

It really was a frantic three days, with the teachers herding the students from one attraction to the next. The constant shrill of the whistle and the shouting of, "Pali-wha" (come quickly) to encourage the students to move along as quickly as possible. We saw incredible scenery like caves, rock pools, mountains and even had the opportunity to go up the mountain in a cable car. On the final day, we went to a look-out tower on the border between North and South Korea and then it was back to the hotel for lunch. As with all *good things, they must come to an end. We left the hotel and travelled to the end of the road. The road was lined with all the hotel staff that had served us. They bowed graciously in an act of thanks and waved to us, as each of the buses passed by them. It was a fitting end to a marvellous journey.*

Another kind of meeting that you will be expected to attend is the school's sports day. There are no formal teaching classes on this day, but again a great opportunity to bond with teachers and students alike. Many of the teachers get involved with the cheer leading and supporting of their homeroom classes. Invariably there will also be a teachers' race on the day. Teachers from each grade put a team together consisting of an equal number of male and female runners, and then they compete against each other. This race causes much excitement amongst the students as they want their favourite teachers to win. The day would not be complete without the teachers going to dinner and doing some more bonding over a couple of bottles of soju.

Way of the Chicken Warrior

If Superman and a duck had to have a tug of war competition, who would win? The duck of course. Well, that's the way it played out at our school sports day on Monday. Every year the students dress up in their various outfits for the school sports day. Superman was there, as well as a duck, students in pajamas, and an assortment of outfits using face paint, big bow ties and Mickey Mouse ears on their heads.

I was a spectator for the day and had the privilege of sitting in the VIP section. Well, at least I thought it was because the Principal, Vice-Principal and sports administration staff were there. On second thoughts, it could have been the OTA section - Overweight Teachers Area. Besides the sports officials and the pregnant teachers, there was only me. You're probably asking (or not) why I was not participating in this auspicious event? If you must know, I sustained an injury during the recent Super 14 rugby final at Loftus Versfeld in Pretoria. I don't want to mislead you into thinking that I played in the final (I know some of you were thinking that), but when the Bulls scored their eighth try, I vigorously punched the air with my index finger and sustained serious ligament damage to that finger. Hence, my inability to take part in two of the main events, tug-of-war and rope jumping (skipping).

Now I can hear many of you saying what kind of sports day is this? Where's the athletics? But let me tell you, this ranks right up there with Super 14 rugby. Admittedly, no-one was sin binned and sent off the field, but the amount of injuries sustained during the first few encounters of tug-o-war and skipping was phenomenal. Students came hobbling, limping, clutching and holding various parts of their body, when entering the "OTA." The amount of bandages and plasters that were being administered was incredible. A pharmaceutical company would have been a proud (and very rich) sponsor. There was even a stretcher propped up against the wall and I was hoping this was not an ominous sign of things to come.

The day wore on and I was starting to get a bit bored with the monotony of the events and the continual 'quacking' of the duck team as to how good they were. Then I heard someone say it was time for the chicken fighting. I thought to myself, how barbaric and how can they expose these little kids to something like this?

The PE teacher was busying using chalk and laying out a huge circle on the field. The "chickens" would then fight from within the confines of the circle. I thought to myself,

"Clucking hell, these chickens must be pretty big to need such a huge circle." As it turns out, they don't use live chickens. Mind you, they don't use dead ones either. Teams of students go into the circle and one half stands on the one side of the circle and the other in the other half and then they compete against each other. However, before you can 'peck' a fight with anyone, you have to assume the chicken stance. Now this looks like something out of a karate kid movie. Although, you don't have some ancient Chinese kung-fu guru in the background, using child labour to do his chores under the pretext of showing them how to move their arms and hands in martial arts movements – wax on, wax off, wax on, wax off. It's really quite simple. You stand on one leg and then bring your other leg up and cross it over the leg that you're standing on. You then rest the crossed leg on the standing legs thigh. Then you hold the crossed leg's foot and begin to hop around.

Now I am a natural at this, as I have had lots of practice. Just the other night I was walking around barefoot in my apartment, when I stubbed my toe on the door frame. I immediately assumed the chicken fighting stance. To say I was 'hopping' mad would be an understatement. I was yelling (might even have been yodelling) expletive words that included mother and I think a trucker. So I have the experience of the stance, as well as the war cry.

The rules are that you have to stay inside the circle and to assume the stance at all times. The idea being that you hop around and try and unbalance your opponent by using your crossed leg as leverage or as in most cases, a battering ram. Once you have been "unbalanced" you have to leave the circle. At the end of a certain time period, the teams with the most people still in the circle are declared the winners. There are also teachers who act as referees to ensure that there is no 'fowl' play.

It was interesting to see how these kids developed their own "war" strategies. The guys would be the first to make the forays into the enemy's territory, while the girls just hung back in their little groups lining the inside of the circle. I assume this is where the term "hen party" comes from. However, the guys caught onto this and soon were playing human ten-pin bowling. They would launch themselves at the first girl and that would have a knock-on effect, taking out a few others as well.

Let's not forget the "kamikaze" chicken fighter. They're the ones that launch themselves at their opponents with little care for the outcome. All they want to do is unbalance their opponent, even if it means taking themselves out of the game. One kid tried this with disastrous effect. He built up speed and flung himself at his opponent. This kid had obviously seen the movie, "The Rocky Horror Picture show," starring Tim Curry and took Tim's advice – "It's just a jump to the left." This poor ex-kamikaze chicken fighter launched himself at thin air. I think I heard him say, "Paaaaaaaaak" before he hit the dirt.

Things can get a little out of hand at times. One kid was

rammed and lay on his back on the ground laughing at his misfortune. At the same time another kid had lost his balance and had fallen onto the kid lying on his back. It looked like something out of Wrestle Mania. It's not as if this guy was so heavy that he got up and the other guy who was lying down, was now stuck between his butt cheeks. However, he wasn't light either. Teachers straightened him out on the ground and started pumping his arms and legs. Other teachers were running over to him with water and towels. I took one look at the guy lying out on the field, glanced across at the stretcher propped up against the wall, and then looked at the guy lying out in the field again. I began to move slowly and quietly to the opposite side to the stretcher. After all, I had injured my index finger and was in no condition to be hauling stretchers around the place!

The afterschool programme or "English Club" is something else for which you may also be responsible. This programme takes place after normal school hours. Your regular school hours may not cover your weekly contractual hours and this programme will help bridge that gap. The duration of these lessons can be anything from between one and two hours long. The lessons could be everyday or once a week. It will depend on your weekly shortfall of contractual hours or the specific needs of your school. You will find that the classes are smaller than your regular classes with anything between five and twenty or more students participating. There is a strong possibility that you will not have a co-teacher to assist you and you will have to teach solo. However, the good news is that the students' English abilities are generally higher in these classes. As the students volunteer for this programme, they may be more motivated to learn English, hopefully resulting in less of a problem with classroom discipline. I was allowed to teach anything in my afterschool programme and did not have to use an assigned textbook. This allowed me to be creative and make the lessons a bit more challenging for the students. My students tended to be more relaxed around me in the afterschool programme and it was a nice opportunity to bond with them further. Should you be one of the fortunate ones where your weekly contractual hours are being met, you will be paid overtime for the hours accumulated during the afterschool programme. If this is the case, it's strongly advised that you keep copies of your lesson plans and attendance registers. The Education Department can be very bureaucratic when it comes to paperwork and they will need these documents in order to effect payment.

There will also be times when adhoc duties and responsibilities may be required to be carried out by the foreign teacher. One such time is during exams for middle and high school students. I was asked to help out with the oral exams for the semester. The students are given a set of standard questions and responses that they learned during the semester. For example, the question might be, "Where are you from?" and the standard response would be, "I am from South Korea." The students would have to learn all of the questions and responses prior to the oral exam. I would then ask each student five questions and they would have to give me the correct responses to each question. They would be evaluated on accuracy and pronunciation for each question. The points would be added up and converted to a percentage. This would then be the students mark for their end of semester oral exam. The process was far from perfect. I had students whose English abilities were very low, but because they had been able to memorise well or selected the easier questions, they received higher percentages than those whose English abilities were much higher. Other examination related duties may include monitoring the students while they are taking the exam. During school exams you will not be teaching any classes, so this would be a welcome relief from the boredom of sitting behind your desk. You will not be required to assist the students if they ask any questions, but to ensure that they don't get the examination answers from sources other than their own heads. Students and parents alike are quite fanatical about attaining good marks at school. They are prepared to have meetings with the department head, as well as the relevant subject teacher, just to fight over a mark or two. There is tremendous pressure on the teacher setting the exam to ensure that the exam paper is hundred percent correct. It is for this reason that the English teacher setting the exam may ask you to edit the exam paper. You will not only ensure that the questions are grammatically correct and unambiguous, but also that the answers are correct.

CHAPTER 5

HELPFUL HINTS

KOREAN LANGUAGE

"Those who know nothing of foreign languages, knows nothing of their own." – Johann Wolfgang von Goethe

I don't want to state the obvious here, but one of the first things that you will notice when you arrive in Korea is that they speak Korean and not English. Small day to day chores that you used to do in your home country can now become more time consuming and frustrating. A trip to the local convenience store to buy washing detergent or floor cleaner is no longer a simple task of going to the correct aisle, reading the label on the product and then placing it in your shopping cart. All of the product labels and product information are written in Hangeul. Hangeul is the writing system used by Koreans. You are probably thinking, "No problem. I will look at the pictures." This doesn't always work out as the picture sometimes is misleading and you don't really know what the product is used for or contains. Now you certainly wouldn't want a situation where you think you are buying shampoo when in fact it could be paint stripper! Although, when you do figure out that you have bought paint stripper, it will certainly explain the hair loss. There is also only so much scratching, sniffing and shaking of product contents that one can do before the shopkeeper becomes a little concerned that they might have a loony person in their establishment. Now I am not for one minute suggesting that you rush out and try and learn the Korean language before coming to Korea. If you can or have already, that is wonderful. It will now give you an opportunity to immerse yourself in the language while teaching in Korea. However, it is not necessary and you will certainly be able to survive without it, if you so choose. The good news is that Koreans are very eager for you to learn their language and you will never have to worry about finding a tutor to teach you. In all probability you will also find that your local office of education will also arrange Korean lessons for you. One thing that I can recommend is that you learn the basic language structure of Hangeul. This will enable you to read and pronounce words, even though you might not understand what you are reading or saying. What's the point of learning the structure then? It is pointless buying a phrase book and using it if your pronunciation is all wrong, as it could mean something totally different. I mean you wouldn't want to ask a person if you could use their toilet, when in fact the way you pronounced it, you were asking to sleep with their daughter! I know that it's an exaggerated example, but I remember when I was travelling on a long distance bus and needed the toilet. When the bus pulled up at a scheduled stop, I asked in what I thought was perfect Korean, where the toilets were. I just got blank stares. It was only when they saw my swift feet shuffling, flaying arms and tensed look on my face that they realised that I needed the toilet. Fortunately for me they didn't think I was doing a Mohamed Ali impersonation. The other useful thing about learning the structure of the language is that you are able to read signs. This becomes invaluable when travelling local or long distance. It becomes a little embarrassing when you are asking for directions or where a place is and you find that you're standing right under a signboard that gives you those directions or next to the place that you're actually looking for. There is a wonderful book called, "Yes, You Can Learn Korean Language Structure in Forty Minutes," written by Tongku Lee (ISBN: 978-1-56591-091-1). It is a very easy book to read and understand. It covers the Korean alphabet (characters), consonants, vowels and how words are formed through the combination rules for vowels and consonants. Buy the book and read it during your flight to Korea and you should have it waxed by the time you land in Korea, presuming your flight is longer than forty minutes, that is.

HEALTH

"Eh, what's up doc?" – Bugs Bunny

One thing that you really want to look after when you are in a foreign country is your health. You don't want to have to go to hospitals, dentists or General Practitioners (GP's) unless it is totally necessary. Don't get me wrong, there is absolutely nothing wrong with South Korea's healthcare system. In fact, according to the Ministry of Health and Welfare website, Korea is one of the most advanced countries in healthcare in Asia. An article in the Korea Herald (8/7/2010) also stated that more than sixty thousand foreigners came to Korea for medical purposes in 2009. The article went on to say that the amount of medical tourists had doubled in the last two years. If these facts don't instil confidence in their ability, then give some thought to the following. The quality of healthcare that is provided in South Korea is managed by the government through a strict evaluation and hospital accreditation programme. Korea also carries out the largest number of clinical trials around the world. More importantly, all hospitals are not-for-profit organisations. Therefore, hospitals aren't concerned with the cost, but their priority is rather on the patient and the quality of service they deliver to the patient. One of the big differences between Korean and a Western healthcare system is that there isn't a private GP system. You have to go to hospital for everything. The reason why I mentioned earlier that you should try and avoid having to go to a medical practitioner, is that it can become quite frustrating because of the language barrier. The last thing one wants to do is play charades and name association games when trying to explain to the doctor what your symptoms are, especially while experiencing unbearable pain. I speak from experience.

Whilst in Korea I had to go to hospital on more than one occasion. On the first occasion I had to have a pterygium (Surfer's eye) surgically removed from my eye. The doctor had a smattering of English, but gave up trying to explain what he was going to be doing and just carried on with the surgery. Doesn't sound scary, until he wants to stick an injection needle in your eye to anaesthetize it or cut your eye with a scalpel and peel back a layer so he can scrape off the pterygium. On another occasion I was admitted into ER, where numerous MRI scans, medication and Extracorporeal Shock Wave Lithotripsy (ESWL) were administered for kidney stones. I mention these two examples to obviously highlight the need to take your co-teacher or someone with you who can translate into Korean for you. I also want to point out that these are not minor health issues and they were not only professionally done, but also done at a fraction of the cost that it would have been done in my home country. According to the website Medical Korea, you will find that medical costs are about twenty to thirty percent of the costs that they charge in the United States. It has also been over a year since I had my procedures done and there has been no recurrence of the symptoms to date. Hopefully this will alleviate some of the anxiety you may have about using healthcare in South Korea.

The good news is that in the event of you becoming ill, you will be covered by your medical insurance scheme, as per your school contract. You pay fifty percent and your employer pays fifty percent towards your health insurance. Your portion amounts to 4,77% of your gross salary. Your co-teacher or supervisor will normally arrange your health insurance card for you when you first arrive. You will have to submit copies of your Alien Registration Card (ARC) and passport. The application will take about one to two weeks to be processed. Should you require medical treatment, you should take your Health Insurance Card and ARC with you to the hospital or clinic. This will ensure that you will be covered for medical insurance. In the event that you forget to take your health insurance card, give the hospital your full name and ARC number and they will be able to do a search on their computers for your health insurance card number.

Should you have a medical or any other emergency, you can dial 119. Just to clarify that needing to go to the toilet is not classified as an emergency, although a fire is. If you are calling from a landline, your location will automatically be identified and there will be no need to worry about the language, as translation services are available. To locate a hospital, just look for a green cross on a building. This is opposed to a red cross like we have in the West. There are hospitals that have doctors that can understand and speak English, but it is still a good idea to take your co-teacher along with you in order to ease any communication difficulties. If for whatever reason your co-teacher or a Korean translator cannot accompany you, it would be best if you ask them to recommend a suitable English speaking medical professional to whom you can go. There is also nothing wrong with going into one of the many Facebook groups in South Korea and asking other English foreigners for a referral.

You can find out more about Medical insurance at http://www.nhic.or.kr/wbe/index.html

Kidney Stones

It was Monday morning and the start of another long week. I hadn't been feeling well the night before and I thought I was coming down with flu. I had a huge headache with nausea and had incredible pain in the right lower side of my stomach. I decided that I wasn't going to take chances with this new H1N1 flu and asked my co-teacher to take me to hospital. The doctor did his poking and prodding and suspected Appendicitis. He wanted to take blood and some x-rays. After having done that, he told me they couldn't find my appendix. Well, so much for the Appendicitis. He said that I should monitor the symptoms and if they continued, I should come back again.

The following morning, the headache, nausea and pain had increased beyond bearable limits. We rushed off to

hospital and went to the ER. A doctor examined me and the next thing I knew I was hooked up to a drip and being given an injection. I was told further x-rays and other tests were needed. About three hours later after all the tests were done, I had another session with the doctor. I was told that I had a 6,25mm kidney stone in my right kidney. Apparently, any stone over 5mm requires medical intervention. The thought of an operation and having to spend time in a Korean hospital scared the hell out of me.

Let me put things in context here. A Korean hospital is run a little differently to a traditional Western hospital. There are nurses, but the majority of them work an eight to five day. Obviously they have skeleton staff that takes care of emergencies. However, if you are recovering in a Korean hospital, your family takes care of you – no nurses! Furthermore, there are no meals that are brought to you; you need to provide your own. In other words, all after care is the responsibility of your family. The other noticeable thing is that Korean hospitals are not as spacious as Western hospitals, with very little privacy. The space between the hospital beds is probably less than 0,5m. Two people standing back to back in the space between two beds would find it a tight squeeze. The other thing that I noticed while lying on one of the beds in my pain, drug-filled haze was the amount of beds that had dried blood stains running down the sides of them. I assumed this was from where the patients' drips had come unstuck. As terrible as all of this sounds, I would rather spend time in a Korean hospital just to get rid of the pain. One person had this to say about the pain of having a kidney stone, "Imagine someone punching you in the stomach, kicking you in the groin and then stabbing you numerous times with an ice pick. When you can imagine this type of pain, multiply it by ten!"

As 'luck' would have it, I would not require any surgery. I was to undergo Extracorporeal Shock Wave Lithotripsy (ESWL). It costs around $450 (W530 000) and uses microwave shock waves to shatter the kidney stone into smaller pieces, so that it may pass easily through the system. If you're lucky, it will work first time around, otherwise you have to have repeated sessions at $450 a pop. I was given two more injections for the pain and then sent to the room where I would receive my ESWL treatment. I lay down on the table while the doctor was pulling me this way and that way to try and position me over the 'sensor'. He started the machine up and it started making this gentle whirring sound. I thought this was nice and soothing. The doctor walked around the machine a few times and then left the room. I could have sworn he locked the door...although the drugs could have made me imagine it. The initial pain that I experienced was excruciating. Imagine that your kidney is a piñata and the excited kid with the baseball bat is the machine and the kid is repeatedly bashing the piñata to try and get the candy. This is what was happening to me. The machine was repeatedly 'shooting' these microwave shock waves directly at the kidney, trying to smash the kidney stone. At one point the doctor sent in my co-teacher to tell me to breathe normally and stop holding my breath as the treatment wouldn't work. He knew if he came in and told me, I would have probably given him a quick sharp ninja kick to his groin. The pain was so intense that I was holding my breath trying to brace myself for the next wave of attack! The *whole process lasted about forty minutes, although it seemed like forty years. At the end of the session I felt like a million bucks. No headache, nausea or pain…the drugs had definitely kicked in!*

It has been almost a week now and I still have not passed the kidney stone. The pain comes and goes and one just has to try and manage it the best way you can. I'm due back at the doctors in a day or two to check whether the stone has passed through my system or not. If not, they want to do another ESWL treatment. There is an English expression, "Once bitten twice shy." They've made my right kidney a piñata once before. I think I will give it a miss this time around and try some natural home remedies…if the pain will let me!

BANKS

"Show me the money!" – Jerry Maguire

The currency for South Korea is the won. The bank notes are issued in four denominations of a 1000 won, 5000 won, 10 000 won and a more recently introduced 50 000 won note. There are also four coin denominations of 500 won, 100 won, 50 won and 10 won. Major foreign credit cards like American Express, MasterCard and Visa are accepted by hotels and other tourist facilities. You will also find that at some of the major Korean banks ATM's they will accept international credit cards. Before leaving your home country, I would find out what the cost of these transactions would be, as you could end up paying high transaction fees for the privilege. Your best bet is to open a Korean bank account as soon as you possibly can. Speaking of which …

One of the first things you should do when arriving in Korea is to open a bank account. To open a bank account you will need your passport or Alien Registration Card. The banks are all very similar and one doesn't really have to shop around to see which one will give the best deal. That being said, I would suggest that you use one of the bigger banks in Korea that have a special foreigner's service. Some of you might be in a rural area and use one of the smaller banks, but when you take a trip into the city those banks might be very scarce and you will have to pay higher transaction fees to use another bank. Five banks that are well represented in most areas throughout Korea are Hana Bank, Kookmin Bank (KB), Korea Exchange Bank (KEB), Nonghyup Bank (NH) and Shinhan Bank. To find out a little more about these banks and the services they offer, please go to their websites.

Hana Bank	http://www.hanabank.co.kr
Kookmin Bank	http://www.kbstar.com
Korea Exchange Bank	http://www.keb.co.kr
Nonghyup Bank	http://www.nonghyup.com
Shinhan Bank	http://www.shinhan.com

The banks trading hours are from 09h00 to 16h30 on weekdays and they are closed on weekends. Many banks will have English forms, as well as staff that can speak English, but there would be no harm in asking your co-teacher to accompany you when going to open a bank account. This is beneficial for a number of reasons. Firstly, this will certainly eliminate any potential problems that you may encounter when opening your bank account. Secondly, having your co-teacher around will also make it easier once your account is opened because they can then show you how to use your ATM card and bank book. Thirdly, many of the queries from foreign teachers on internet social networking sites and message boards are about how to transfer money from Korea back to their home countries. They only think of this a month or two down the line and then become frustrated when they go into the bank and can't seem to explain what they want to do. Being aware of this upfront and having your co-teacher with you, will allow you to communicate this effectively to your bank. They will then be able to set up your bank account in such a way that will enable you to do money transfers when you are ready. It is a good idea to speak with your bank in your home country before you leave, and find out exactly what the requirements are for transferring money back to them. I'm sure each country will have their own set of rules and procedures. Check out the Korean bank websites mentioned earlier to see what their requirements are with regards to this. Many a foreign teacher, including myself, encountered problems when trying to transfer money home for the first time. I ended up doing a wire transfer which cost me a lot of unnecessary admin fees and commissions. The banks could not wire transfer the money in my currency. They first had to convert won to dollars, transfer the money to my home country and then convert the dollars into my home country's currency. A simpler and more cost effective solution would have been internet banking. (Internet banking will also allow you to pay your utility bills like electricity and gas. You can transfer your won into your home country's bank account and it will reflect the equivalent in your country's currency). Should you need to do wire transfers from Korea for whatever reason, remember that you can negotiate for a better exchange rate with the bank. Keep in mind that Korean exchange laws only allow you to transfer a maximum amount of money to your home country per annum. This amount was W20 million, but you will have to check with the Korean banks for the current amount. The higher the amount you are transferring, the more negotiating power you have. From time to time you are going to want to know how much your Korean won is worth in your own currency. A good currency converter website that I found useful was: http://www.xe.com

Besides your own Korean banks ATM's, there are also non-bank ATM's. Non-bank ATM's are not branded any specific bank, which means they will accept most branded banks ATM cards. These non-bank ATM's can be found at convenience stores or in subway stations. If you need to go into the bank for a 'face to face' transaction, remember to take your bank card, Alien Registration Card and/or passport. There is no queuing in Korean banks. When you walk into the bank you will take a numbered ticket. Each teller has a LED screen next to them which displays the number of the next person to be assisted. When your number is displayed, you can go to that teller and they will assist you with your query.

SHOPPING

"Whoever said money can't buy happiness simply didn't know where to go shopping." – Bo Derek

Just like in the West, South Korea has a great variety of shops where one can go shopping. They have everything from huge markets, retail outlets, department stores, upmarket shopping malls, down to little convenience stores on just about every street. Some of the familiar supermarkets that you will encounter are E-Mart, Costco, Tesco Homeplus and LotteMart. Generally they will have a range, all be it a bit limited, of Western products like cereals, pasta, coffee, yoghurt, soft drinks, sandwich spreads, etc. There are also more upmarket department stores like Shinsegae and Hyundai Department stores. These stores do tend to import goods from other countries. So if there is something specific you are looking for and you can't find it anywhere else, try one of these stores and you might just find what you're looking for. If you can't make it to one of the retail stores before it closes, which is highly unlikely because they close quite late, you could always go to a convenience store which is bound to be within walking distance of your apartment. Some of the popular convenience stores are GS, 7-11, Family Mart and Buy the Way. Not really a place to buy Western food, but you will be able to get the basics like bread, milk, sugar and eggs. Just enough basics to get you through to the next day when you can then go to a retail store to replenish your stock. Western food tends to be a little pricier than Korean food. So it will be more cost effective if you can eat what the Koreans eat. If you are really desperate for Western food or want something in particular and can't find it anywhere in Korea, there are quite a few expats in Korea who have started to import goods from the English speaking countries. Do an internet search on Facebook for them or go to one of the Facebook groups that I mention in the "Socialising" section of this chapter. The Arabic communities have set up foreign food markets in places such as Itaewon and Hannam-dong. They are a great place to stock up on spices, legumes, teas, etc. For an interesting website all about Korean food and tips for ex-pats living in Korea, go to http://www.zenkimchi.com

I have attached a breakdown of the costs for basic Western foodstuffs. This will give you a rough indication of the cost of living in South Korea. Remember though, it will be cheaper if your diet is similar to that of the Koreans. To convert prices to your currency, go to http://www.xe.com

My shopping basket

Item	Quantity	Price
Bacon	260g	W5 950 – W7 100
Beverages:		
Beer	355ml x 6	W7 260
	1,6L	W3 800
Bottled water	2L	W440 – W830
Coffee	100g	W5 680
	Box of sachets x 50	W5 120

Soft drinks	1,8L Coke	W1 950
Tea	Box	Korean W1 800
		Western W3 500
Wine	Yellow Tail 750ml	W12 000
	Table Mountain 750ml	W8 900 – W12 000
Bread	700g	W1 500
	380g	W1 450
Butter / Margarine	400g	W6 580
Cereal	Kellogg's Flakes 500g	W5 510
	All Bran 450g	W5 350
Cheese	Camembert 100g	W5 800
	Brie 100g	W5 800
Fruit:		
Apples	x 6	W4 980
Bananas	100g	W398
Kiwis	x 12	W6 480
Pineapple	x 1	W3 480
Milk	1L	W1 980
Pasta	Spaghetti 500g	W2 520

	Macaroni 500g	W2 520
Sauces:		
BBQ	510g	W3 350
Mayonnaise	800g	W3 190 – W4 950
Pasta	685g	W4 300
Tomato	800g	W2 780
Vegetables:		
Carrots	1kg	W2 980
Cucumber	x 2	W2 680
Lettuce	x 1	W1 980
Potatoes	800g	W1 680
Tomatoes	500g	W5 480

There are also specialist markets like Nam-dae-mun, Dong-dae-mun and Insa-dong, which are all located in Seoul. Nam-dae-mun and Dong-dae-mun are the two biggest markets in Korea and sell things like folk artefacts, clothing, produce, everyday necessities and accessories. Insa-dong market has traditional tea houses, antiques, ceramics, paper stores and galleries. Even though prices are very low, they can still be negotiated, so be sure to ask for discount. If you are big on electronic gadgets, then I-Park

Mall is definitely the place to go to. It has floors and floors of electronics from digital cameras through to computers and notebooks. I-Park Mall is situated at Yongsan Station in Seoul. Some days you might feel homesick and crave for something Western. COEX mall is the antidote for that homesickness. It is Asia's largest underground shopping mall and covers an area of 85 000 m². It has hundreds of shops, two food courts, a cinema complex, large bookstore and an aquarium. COEX is located in the World Trade Centre complex in Gangman District, Seoul. For more info, go to http://www.coex.co.kr/eng

"Can I Have a Discount, Please?"

With the weekend fast approaching, I was starting to consider what my options were. I had been eyeing out the latest Samsung HMX-H106 camcorder and was considering a "shopping trip" to Seoul. The trip would certainly be worth it if I could get my hands on one of those camcorders. It can record up to 64GB of video. That's ten hours of filming! That's a lot of footage of you and your mates making a fool of yourselves while under the influence of alcohol! It just so happened that I had also popped off an email to a local radio station, to ask if I could be a guest on their show. Why? Hey, it seemed like a good idea at the time! Besides, so many of my friends had told me that I have a face for radio. I'm bound to be a success. The radio station called to say that they had cancelled the interview, but could I come through to Seoul as the producer would like to talk to me. That settled it. I was going to Seoul this weekend.

I dragged myself out of bed and managed to get to the bus terminal by 07h30. As luck would have it, the bus was

fairly empty and I had managed to secure a seat right at the back of the bus. I was just getting settled in when a woman came to sit next to me. She said, "I know you." Your mind immediately starts racing to think where in the heck you had met this person and just hope that it wasn't on one of those nights where you were a little under the weather and you thought you were God's gift to everything! It turns out that she is the sister of one of the Korean teachers who attended my teachers' workshop. I had also been at a dinner where she was present. We got chatting and discussed what we wanted to do in the future. She said that she was studying to be an interpreter, as she could no longer get into hosting television shows because she failed her screen test. I mentioned that I was going to talk to a radio producer in Seoul and the fact that I wanted to develop my voice and learn not to speak so fast. She said that I was slow. Now I'm not too sure if she was implying that I was mentally challenged, whether she wanted me to take advantage of her and I was not complying, or whether she felt that the speed of my voice was fine and I did not need to do any work on slowing it down. I made the assumption she was referring to my voice. After all, this was only about a ninety minute bus trip and I wouldn't have enough time to argue the other assumptions.

    I arrived at the Express Bus Terminal and made my way down to the subway to catch a train to Yongsan. Yongsan has this huge electronics store where you can buy electronic goods at very good prices. That's if you can negotiate of course! This time I came prepared. I had chatted to a friend of mine about negotiating with these guys and he gave me the low down on how to do it. Whatever the asking price is, you offer them fifty percent less. You then start to haggle about the price. After a while you ask them if that's their final price, then you still offer a lower figure. Once you've both agreed on a price, you then ask them about "service". Now service in their terms is extras like another battery, tripod, bag, extra memory, etc. You have to be on your toes, because these guys could sell ice to an Eskimo. However, I was at an advantage. After all, there is no ice or Eskimo's in South Korea.

I was confident when I arrived at the I-Park Mall. I walked around and started doing my "negotiating". I had managed to knock about twenty percent off the price of a camcorder. However, things were going a bit slow. I decided to go in for the kill. I walked up to the guy selling camcorders and with my best Korean accent said, "Ka ka juseyo." By the look he gave me, you'd swear I had just said something nasty about his mother. Now I know ka ka juseyo sounds like something that your mother might have said to you when you were younger. While crawling around on the ground trying to put snails and worms in your mouth, your mother would say, "No, ka ka! Don't put in your mouth." However, ka ka juseyo basically means that you want a discount. It didn't seem like these guys were going to budge, so I decided to give it a break and go for lunch.

I decided to go to Joe's Sandwich bar for a bite to eat. They make an incredible club sandwich and have coffees to die for. For about W5300 you get a club sandwich and a cappuccino – definitely value for money in my book. To be honest, I have become addicted to their coffees. I would gladly pay W5300 just for the coffee alone. I was the only customer in the store and while I was munching on my club sandwich, the store owner just walked out of the store and left me alone there. You might say, "Big deal, what's the issue?" But it's like leaving an alcoholic in a bottle store by himself and expecting him not to drink any alcohol. I love coffee. Needless to say, the owner came back after five minutes and I had managed to restrain myself or maybe my friend on the bus was right...I'm a little slow. However, if this happened to someone else in the West, I'm sure the store owner would have come back to the store finding nothing more than a few shop-fittings left.

I made my way back to the I-Park mall to continue my negotiating. I spoke to so many salesmen before lunch that it was a mission to try and remember to whom I spoke and what price we had agreed upon. I think they realised this – my wondering around aimlessly must have been a dead give-away. I had to start negotiating all over again. Though, this time around they started confusing me by telling me the price was also influenced by where the product was made. If it's made in China, it's cheaper than if it's made in Korea. It just so happens that this particular model is only made in Indonesia! I decided that I was rather going to hang on to my hard earned Won and do a little more research before I outlay a huge wad of cash on something that might not be of the highest quality. So it looks like the saying "buyer beware" has some credibility here!

After that long and tedious day of negotiating there was nothing left to do, but for me to go home. I jumped on the first available bus and made my ninety minute journey back to the familiarity of my little town. No ice, no Eskimos, no salesmen...perfect!

TRAVEL

"Been there done that and got the T-shirt."

This part of the book is not meant to be seen as a comprehensive travel guide. It is far from that and the purpose is to only give you a brief overview of travel in South Korea. If you are looking for a comprehensive guide, I would suggest a book like the "Lonely Planet."

South Korea is within easy access to all the continents of the world. Its location makes it ideal for you to use as your base and to travel to other countries for short or extended holidays. It is also reasonably affordable to travel from South Korea. Most Koreans like to go abroad for their vacations and due to this demand for travel, it brings down the cost of flights and accommodation. It is also very cheap to travel within the borders of South Korea as well. South Korea's transportation network is very extensive, making travel throughout the country relatively easy.

- Public Transportation

If you are living in a city, subways are one of the quickest ways to get around. Subway lines go to all the major train stations, bus terminals and popular areas. One can buy subway tickets at ticket vending machines or a ticket window near the entrance to the subway platform. Frequent commuters can buy a T-money card. This is a card loaded with a credit of a pre-determined amount of money. Each time the commuter swipes the card through the turnstile, the cost of the trip is automatically deducted from the credit. When the credit is used up, you then purchase more credits. It works out a little cheaper to buy a money card than to purchase an individual ticket each time. It is also far more convenient, as you don't have the hassle of having to buy a ticket each time you want to take the subway. The subway maps are colour coded and very easy to follow. There is no reason to worry about missing your stop either. On each platform is written the name of the station, as well as the station you have just come from and the next station you are going to. Furthermore, announcements about the upcoming stops are first given in Korean and then in English. Some subways will also have LED boards in them to indicate what the upcoming stop is.

There is also a train service that links all the major South Korean cities. The KTX is South Korea's high speed train that travels at a speed of 300km/h or more. It is definitely worth experiencing a ride on this train. Tickets can be bought online. To find out more about the KTX service, go to http://www.korail.com

South Korea also has inner city and long distance bus services. It is relatively cheap and safe. I used to travel on a regular basis on the long distance buses. I travelled 170km from my little town into Seoul at least once a month. The cost of the one-way fare was about W10 000.

Taxis are also used extensively in South Korea. There is normally a minimum charge and this does vary from city to city. Sometimes I would take the taxi from my apartment to the bus terminal to catch the long distance bus. It is a distance of about 3km and it cost me around W3800. Every taxi has a meter on the dashboard and at the end of your journey one only need look at the meter to see what your fare will be. It's always best to carry cash, as many taxis might not accept credit cards. Some taxis do accept the T-money card. Should you require a receipt; the taxi driver will be able to give you one.

As mentioned in an earlier chapter, Incheon Airport is the eighth busiest airport. Korea has two major airlines, Korean Air and Asiana. Both airlines offer international and domestic flights. There are around fifteen Korean cities which have air links with each other. The nice thing about flying within South Korea is that the flights are never longer than an hour in duration. So it literally is a hop, skip and jump to wherever you want to go within Korea. You will find that there is a bus service that caters for trips to and from your city to the airport.

For more detailed information on subways (maps, fares, etc), buses (routes, fares, etc), flights and ferry schedules, go to http://traffic.visitkorea.or.kr/lang/en

Trains, Planes and Automobiles

It was Benjamin Disraeli who said, "Like all great travellers, I have seen more than I remember, and remember more than I have seen." For the last week or so, I have been exploring the East coast of South Korea and feel just like Mr Disraeli. It was me, my friends, my backpack and the open road. Over the course of our trip, we saw many fascinating and wonderful things. There was far too much to be able to cover in one little story.

Our trip started with a one and a half hour bus ride to Seoul, the capital of South Korea. A further four hour bus ride ensued, to a city called Sokcho on the East coast of South Korea. Over the course of two days, we were to experience and take in some wonderful scenes and

memories. Whilst there, we hiked through Seoraksan National Park, saw a rather large bronze Buddha and managed to ride their famed cable car. We had timed our arrival in Sokcho perfectly, as they were hosting a free two hour summer music festival. On the night we went to watch the concert, it was pouring with rain. This did not stop the promoters, musicians or the fans from coming. Instead of cancelling the concert, the event organisers handed out plastic raincoats to everyone. Even though the grounds where the concert was held had turned to mud, and the fact that most of the audience had become soaked to the bone, including myself, everyone stuck around to hear the musicians perform.

The next day another long distance bus trip ensued. We steadily made our way down the East coast to a little port town called Donghae. This is where we were to catch our ferry, the Sea Flower, to take us to Ulleungdo the next day. We stayed in what the Koreans call a 'pension'. This was to be our first night of many, where we would sleep on the floor and have refreshing cold showers. The following day we got on our ferry, the Sea Flower, and spent just over three hours before we reached Ulleungdo. We spent two amazing days on the island, not only seeing the sights, but also living the culture. We did not book into a hotel or motel, but rather opted for a minbak or home stay. A minbak is where you actually stay at a local home and experience their culture. The island also has a cable car which takes you up the mountain to some of the best vantage points to see the island. The total circumference of Ulleungdo is about 56km and I at least managed to cycle a little way around. It is extremely scenic and you are literally on the water's edge as you cycle around. Whilst there, I also managed to visit the famous Dokdo, which is about 87,4km from Ulleungdo. Dokdo is famous because Korea and Japan both insist that the island belongs to them.

Two days later, we were back at Donghae, or Mukho port to be precise. We did not want to relive the 'pension experience' that we had two days earlier and decided to find an alternative place to stay. We eventually managed to find a spa. What we didn't realise is that this was almost like a pension, but on a much larger scale. After spending the night with my fellow travel companions and some two or three hundred other travellers, all in the same open space, it was time for me to part ways and head back home to my hometown. The journey would take some six hours by bus, crisscrossing through South Korea. All in all it was a wonderful holiday and a nice way to recharge the batteries for the upcoming school semester.

So I suppose maybe this article was not about trains, planes and automobiles. More like bicycles, buses and ferries, but at least now I can say, "Been there, done that ... got the T-shirt!"

- Accommodation

There is a wide variety of holiday accommodation available in South Korea. There are hotels, motels, minbak, yo-gwan, pensions, spas and youth hostels. A minbak or home stay is where you get to stay in one of the locals' houses and get a closer look at everyday Korean life. A pension is similar to renting out a fully furnished apartment. However, don't expect to get beds and table and chairs to sit on. In the pension where friends and I stayed, we slept on the floor and just received the basics i.e. microwave, TV, cutlery, pots and pans, etc. As always, the internet is a useful resource for locating and booking accommodation in South Korea. For the most part you will have to get your co-teacher to assist you because most of the sites are in Korean. Alternatively, you could use an English travel agent to do all your bookings for you. Keep in mind that a travel agent will also add their commission onto whatever package that they manage to secure for you. To view some of the youth hostels in South Korea, go to http://www.kyha.or.kr

"I was on Stage with the King"

Yes, that's right. I was on stage with Elvis Presley. It does sound a little weird, since Elvis 'left the building' almost 32 years ago to the day.

We had just come back from a trip to Ulleungdo and Dokdo. These are two islands off the coast of South Korea. The ferry docked at Donghae very late and we had not arranged any accommodation. Fortunately for us, there was a Korean on the ferry who could speak English. She suggested that we stay at the local spa, as this was good, clean accommodation. When I heard the word spa, I had visions of luxury and opulence. After a short taxi ride from the harbour, I arrived at the spa. At the reception counter were these huge mounds of towels and what looked like shorts and T-shirts stacked on the counter. Through my excellent communication skills using a combination of what one can only describe as Pictionary and Charades, I managed to secure a 'room' for the night. This was at a cost of W6000! This is very cheap, considering that your average hotel room costs about four or five times more than that. I began to wonder what I had actually paid for.

Shortly afterwards, my friends arrived with our newly acquired 'interpreter'. It turns out that my 'room' was in fact an open area where many other people could sleep ... about two or three hundred other people! However, even though I was tired, I was up for the adventure. They handed me a towel and a set of clothes or was it prison wear? Blue shorts and T-shirt for the men, pink for the women and green for the children. I was also handed a key with a numbered disc attached to it. I wasn't sure if the number referred to my inmate number or prison cell number. It turns out it was my locker number. You wore the key and disc around your arm or leg like a bracelet. The disc also had some sort of chip in it and if you wanted to purchase anything, they would just swipe the disc and the purchases would be added to your bill. I wasn't buying any of this, so I wasn't going to wear mine, but rather keep my disc and key at arm's length ... just in case I walked into some area I wasn't supposed to be in and I got zapped with a bolt of electricity!

We were informed that we could only take in a small bag, but our backpacks, bicycles, etc. had to remain at reception. They told us not to worry as it was safe. There was CCTV everywhere (including the changing rooms) so no-one could take our stuff. Furthermore, your shoes had to be locked in your locker, as no shoes were allowed inside. Blue uniform, key number, no shoes / shoe laces, belts or personal effects...hhmmm, prison or psychiatric ward?

We finally made our way down to the changing rooms and showers. Whilst getting undressed there was this man *standing with his arms folded, grinning and staring at us. Now, this was just not on. In the Western world, it is an unwritten law amongst men that you don't go around staring at another man's equipment ... unless of course you're that way inclined. With this in mind, gripped with panic, I started to have that scene from the movie 'Deliverance' playing over and over in my mind. You know the one ... weird banjo music in the background and where the hillbilly has a gun pointed at his captives while making them go 'on all fours', as he 'rides' them from behind and tells them to squeak like a pig! On the other hand there is CCTV, so it should be safe. Although, for all I know, all his mates could be sitting on the other side of the camera and shouting, "Yeah, squeaks like a pig!" However, fortune was smiling on us ... not smiling as much as the little man watching us, but smiling none the less. It turns out that he was just waiting for us to get changed so that he could then direct us to where the showers and other facilities were.*

After going down a short flight of stairs, we were in the main area of the spa. In the open area, it looked like an aerobics or yoga workout was about to begin as there were these long gym mats everywhere. I was later to learn that this was the sleeping area and the long gym mats were our beds. Leading off this open area, were two or three little restaurants, a PC room (computer games and internet) and what one can only describe as 'chill' rooms. These 'chill' rooms were sealed air conditioned rooms that one could go and sleep in and always seemed to be popular amongst the 'guests'.

We decided to move away from the crowds and found a nice raised area which they were using as a stage. No need to pitch a tent or make a bed, just drop your gym mat down and that's where you sleep. I was in good company though. There was this life-size statue of Elvis sitting on a bar stool holding a guitar. I assume they were having some sort of tribute to him that week, as it was the anniversary of his death. No sooner had I nodded off to sleep and the crowds started to move in on us. I now understand the comedian, Lenny Henry's explanation as to why men burp, fart, cough and make other loud bodily noises while they sleep. According to him, it goes back to our caveman days. Men had to protect their families in the cave, so they burped, farted and made other loud bodily noises so that animals or their enemies would be too afraid to go into the cave. "Oh, it's not safe to go in there. It sounds like somebody is being murdered or killed!" I felt like doing the same to try and protect my little piece of personal space. I even had two ladies try and muscle in on my area.

It was a restless night's sleep with everyone going to bed at different times, but an experience I can well recommend. Now, where are those two ladies that tried to muscle in on my area? "Love me tender, love me true, all my dreams ..."

- Travel Agents

Your main co-teacher will probably be more than willing to assist you with non-school related stuff, as they know how difficult it is for you to live and work in a foreign country. However, there might be times when they are just too busy with their own work that they are unable to assist you. It will be times like these that knowing of an English travel agent can certainly come in handy. Here are some English travel agents that have been used by foreign teachers in Korea.

Xanadu	Soho Travel	UB Travel Service
http://www.xanadu.co.kr	http://www.sohoholiday.com	
Ms Jenny Lee		Sancho
070 7891 7771	02 322 1713 / 4	070 7596 5977
xanadu@xanadu.co.kr	soho@sohotravel.kr	yonghunkw@gmail.com

- Things they don't tell you about

There is a lot to do and see in Korea no matter what your interests are. To see what's "out there" and to get a better feel of what to expect when you get here, you can go to the official Korean tourism website at http://www.visitkorea.or.kr

There are also some unusual and interesting things that you may or may not get to hear about, but are worth a mention and least going to see or try. One such thing is a 419m² double storey toilet shaped house. It is located in Suwon, which is about 40km south of Seoul. The house is constructed of steel, glass and concrete. It cost its owner, Sim Jae-Duck, a reportedly $1,6 million to build. He said he built the house in order to emphasise the importance of better sanitation in all countries. It's quite a sight to see and if you cannot manage to go and look for yourself, just type in "toilet house" in any internet search engine and there will be a host of pictures and even videos of the toilet house. Haeshindang Park or Penis Park as it is also known is situated along the East coast of Korea in Samcheok, Gangwon Province. The park consists entirely of sculptured phalluses. The park was built based on a legend about a young virgin woman who drowned. It was rumoured that her tormented soul was affecting the fishing in the area as the sea had become barren. To try and appease her spirit the people of the village started carving phalluses and performing rituals. I'm sure you're probably saying, "Tell us more about these rituals," but let's rather continue with the story. After doing this, the fishermen were able to get a good catch. The phallic carvings range from park benches with penis armrests to a penis cannon and even animals of the Chinese zodiac. Another park to visit is World Cup Park also known as Landfill Park. It used to be a landfill site for fifteen years with some ninety two million tons of garbage being dumped there. The site has been rehabilitated and comprises of five smaller parks that make up the World Cup Park. You can play golf, camp, hike along the walkways or just take in the scenery from one of the many viewpoints. The park covers an area of 272 000 m² and is situated in Seoul.

If sightseeing isn't your thing, then why not try some of the Korean delicacies? Silkworm larvae are cooked in large vats and are quite crunchy when eaten. Then there is live baby octopus. Be careful if you decide to try this. A friend of mine decided he was going to indulge in sampling one and told me how the octopus put up a bit of a fight. The suction caps on the octopus tentacles managed to get a grip on his tongue, which made it difficult for him to swallow the little fellow. Well, if sightseeing and sampling Korean delicacies isn't your thing either, what about just relaxing and pampering yourself? If this is the case, then you must go and enjoy a session with Doctor Fish. You place your feet in this huge fish tank and these little fish, known as Doctor Fish, nibble all the dead skin cells off your feet. The session lasts about twenty minutes and you can enjoy a nice refreshing drink while the fish do all the work.

SOCIALISING

"Do you come here often?" – Unknown Author

Being thousands of miles away from home immersed in a different environment and culture will more than likely result in you suffering from some form of culture shock. Added to this is the lack of opportunity to have a decent conversation with someone in English. So at some point you are going to be craving the company of some Westerners. These cravings tend to be a bit more intense if you are in a rural area. Socialising becomes almost a necessity in order to just stay sane. There will be opportunities to socialise with work colleagues at and after work, as well as socialising with other foreigners and people not connected with your school.

Let me start by dealing with socialising with work colleagues. You will find that you will be invited to many lunches, dinners and even colleagues weddings. It is not formally required to go, but it is best to attend these functions, especially if there are a large number of your colleagues going. They see this as part of establishing good work relationships with each other. In the West, we generally frown on colleagues who go out and get plastered at work functions. It is exactly the opposite in South Korea. Many Koreans will drink till they get drunk before leaving the restaurant. I make it sound like they are a bunch of alcoholics, but remember in their culture it is custom to offer someone a friendship drink. They don't really like to drink beer because they don't want to get a beer belly. Soju is their preferred choice. They will offer each other a drink in a shot glass to symbolise that they want to build a friendship or relationship with you. Generally, everyone wants to be everyone's friend and if there are forty of your colleagues around the table, getting drunk is not a journey, it's a destination! By getting drunk together they believe that they build better work relationships. A point I did mention in the culture section, is that once you have accepted the drink, you are to turn your head away from the person who offered you the drink and then drink the drink. This is seen as a sign of respect and good manners. Trust me you would I to turn your head away when you drink. You try drinking one hundred percent diesel fuel and not flinching or pulling any faces. After many "friendship drinks" you would be surprised how many of your colleagues can speak a smattering of English and in fact you might even be surprised at your ability to speak Korean. I must just add that during my two years in Korea and the many work related functions that I attended, the teachers never got out of hand or had to be reprimanded for behaviour unbecoming a teacher. If you have accepted an invitation to go out with some of your colleagues and you're expecting an early night, a quick word of caution. The Koreans tend to do things in three's when it comes to socialising, especially the males. First they will go to dinner and invariably drink copious amounts of soju. After that it's off to the norabang. A norabang is like a karaoke bar where people go and sing. This is very popular in Korea and if you go with your colleagues you can expect to get roped in. They really do put effort into their singing and one would think that it is a "Korea's Got Talent" show. In fact, I'm surprised that marketing companies haven't picked up on some of these useful benefits of drinking large quantities of alcohol. These useful benefits being discovering your singing talent and being able to speak a foreign language. After the singing, it's off to a Hof or coffee bar. So prepare for a long night out. In my first week at school I went out for dinner with the entire staff and we ended up at a norabang. The evening was thoroughly entertaining except for the part where I was coerced into singing Frank Sinatra's "My Way." I was dead sober at the time, so I have no excuse for butchering a perfectly good song. Even the principal was belting out a few Korean songs.

This brings me to socialising with other people outside of your school environment. If you're in a big city like Seoul or Busan there will be more than enough foreigners to socialise with. It tends to become a little lonely if you're stuck out in some of the rural areas. However, there seems to be a huge growth in the amount of English foreign teachers coming to South Korea. When I first arrived in my little town, there were only about ten foreign teachers there. Two years later and there are more than thirty. People will have their own reasons for coming to Korea. Some want to learn a new culture, some want to save money so that they can pay off debt, whilst others just come to try and "find" themselves. Whatever the reason, you're bound to find someone with whom you can bond.

Sounds Foreign to Me

"We all know that people are the same wherever you go. There is good and bad in everyone. We learn to live, we learn to give each other what we need to survive together alive." Well, that's what Paul McCartney wrote about in the song, "Ebony and Ivory." I find this to be so true, especially as a foreigner in a foreign country.

When moving to a foreign country, one can do as much research as one can possibly do. But, no matter how much research you do, one can never really be prepared for the culture shock that one will inevitably experience. I have had friends who have read the 'Lonely Planet' and 'Let's Go' books inside out. They have read the phrase and language books. They have even brought along their own bedding. To no avail, because they still feel like a fish out of water when they arrive in their new country. This is where your fellow foreigners come into play or as Mr McCartney says, "We learn to live; we learn to give each other what we need to survive..." When you meet your fellow travellers for the first time, there is no time for all the normal social political nonsense. How much money do you earn? What car do you drive? Where do you live? You are just thankful that there is someone else who can speak English, and in full sentences I might add, and you bond almost immediately. And yes, there is good and bad in everyone. Some of the foreigners I have met are characters indeed. One night I was at a pub playing pool, this guy came into the bar and made a beeline for the pool table, shouting on top of his voice, "I think I'm gonna kiss all of you guys!" I could also see that he was obviously a "little" under the weather. Of course I wasn't too perturbed, as I had a pool cue in my hand to fend him off with. It turns out he knew all of the people that I was playing pool with. After greeting all his mates, he came over to me and thrust out his hand to shake mine. "Howin," he said. Followed by, "You probably wondering "Howin" the hell I got this name?"

To be honest, I wasn't, but he brought it up. He lives in North America and comes from an Indian background. It's clear that his mission is to have fun and party up a storm while in South Korea – nothing wrong with that.

Then on the flip side of the coin, you have someone like Riley. He teaches English, but in his spare time he also teaches salsa dancing. Like me, he doesn't come from a teaching background and has spent many years in business in England. Even though teaching is what he earns his living from, salsa dancing is where he gets his inspiration and motivation. His salsa dancing mirrors his day to day life. If anything goes wrong in his salsa dancing, he looks to other areas in his life to see what changes he needs to make in order to improve his life. For him, coming to South Korea is more of a spiritual journey than one of wanting to have fun and party up a storm. We have our opinions, our differences, even our sameness and yet we still manage to get along.

It really is great to see how foreigners in a foreign country can get along so well with each other. It's just a pity that we have to go to a foreign country to do so. Wouldn't it be great if we could achieve this without having to leave our own countries? Imagine all the people living life for today. Imagine all the people living life in peace. No, I am not going to break out into song, but you must admit those Beatles guys sure knew how to write meaningful songs. I think the Joker (Jack Nicholson) from the movie, Batman, summed it up about right when he said, "Why can't we all just get along."

The Internet is extremely useful in connecting with other foreigners in South Korea. Fortunately for you, the internet connectivity in South Korea is super fast and cheap. There is a plethora of websites and social media like Facebook, You

Tube and various blogs that cater specifically for people living in South Korea. All you have to do is type in the words, "living in South Korea," in to any internet search engine and you will be astounded at the amount of information and groups that are out there. It is a good idea to do your research and try link up with a few of these sites before you leave your home country. This way you are assured of some "friends" before you even arrive in the country. Some of the groups that I found very useful on Facebook were:

"English teachers in South Korea"

"I teach English in South Korea"

"South Africans in South Korea"

"ESL lesson share"

"EPIK teacher resource center"

Another extremely useful internet application is Skype. Skype enables you to make free internet calls, video calls and send instant messages. It's a great way to communicate with family and friends back home, as well as with people that you have met in South Korea. The application can be downloaded for free at http://www.skype.com

The bigger cities like Seoul and Busan have many night clubs that are frequented by foreigners. Seoul has and continues to have its fair share of top rated musical acts that come and perform, so foreigners will not be starved of live entertainment. Salsa, tango, swing and hip hop are very active in Seoul. The smaller towns might not be able to attract foreign bands, but you will always find a pub or bar that will cater for Westerner's tastes.

Should you wish to know what's happening in and around Korea, there are two newspapers that have English websites. They are The Korea Herald and The Korea Times. Some good magazines to find out what's happening on the entertainment scene are Ten Magazine and Groove. They list a calendar of events happening around Korea, nightlife, interests and dining.

The Korea Times: http://www.koreatimes.co.kr

The Korea Herald: http://www.koreaherald.co.kr

Ten Magazine: http://10magazine.asia/

Seoul Style (Groove): http://www.seoulstyle.com

Are you a Bi-poler?

According to Wikipedia, bipolar is a psychiatric diagnosis that describes a category of mood disorders defined by the presence of one or more episodes of abnormal elevated moods. When I typed in 'bi-poler' it came up with nothing. I then typed the same thing into Google and the results came back the same as 'bipolar'. However, I don't want to know about mood swings or anything to do with psychiatry. I wanted to find out if such a word existed or if I had just made it up. Let me not dwell on this, but more about the word later.

Whenever you wonder through the streets of South Korea, you are bound to come across these candy striped poles outside certain shop windows. Now many years ago in the Western world, these candy striped poles represented a barber shop where a man could go and have a shave and a haircut. It's still pretty much the same here in Korea, but it's just not exclusively for men. The women can also have their hair done as well. Now I had been in South Korea for many months and did not even notice that not all candy striped poles were the same. In fact, I would never have noticed unless one of my friends had pointed it out to me.

To my knowledge, you get two types of candy striped poles here. One that stands by itself outside a shop window, let's call it a uni-pole (one). The other has two single candy striped poles standing side by side; let's call it a bi-poler (two). The single candy striped pole that stands by itself is where you will get a cut and blow for your hair. The two single candy striped poles standing side by side, well let's just say between a cut and blow, you wouldn't get a cut there...and yes, they would probably "love you long time" if you catch my drift. How do I know this? No, I didn't find out the "hard" way – no pun intended! As mentioned earlier, a friend pointed this out to me.

UNI-POLE

BI-POLER

One night we were travelling home from a pub and we drove past these two candy striped poles that were mounted on the side of the building. My friend asked me if I knew what it was. I naively replied that it was a hair salon or barber shop. It's then that he told me that it was a 'house of ill repute' and began to share this anecdote with me. He told me how he and another one of his friends suspected that two of their colleagues had gone to visit one of these places, but were denying it. It just so happened that the very next day the four of them were in the car together and drove past the very place that they suspected their colleagues of going to. My friend turned to his mate and said, "Remember we came here last night and they wanted to charge us W30 000?" To which the suspected 'offender' replied, "W30 000! They charged us W80 000!" Talk about getting your hand caught in the "cookie" jar! Apparently this guy isn't too bright and the fact that he is Irish has nothing to do with it.

Whilst writing this article, I was wondering how I was going to get a picture of the two candy striped poles, as I couldn't remember where exactly we were when we drove past in my friend's car, and it also happened many months ago. That got me thinking. How in the hell did these guys manage to find out about the symbolism of the two candy striped poles in the first place? There is definitely a language barrier – they can't speak Korean and I'm sure they would have had difficulty in trying to find a Korean who could speak English. I suppose it would be back to the good old tried and tested Charades and Pictionary. Although, the animated suggestive pelvic thrusting while holding onto an imaginary person might not equate to you wanting to have sex in their books. For all you know you could end up being rushed off to hospital with suspected muscle spasms or some sort of epileptic fit! The establishment that I managed to photograph was slap bang in the centre of the busiest thoroughfare. So one can appreciate the attention a foreigner would get when trying to take a photo of the said establishment. All I can say is thank heavens for bushes.

Keeping this in mind, if you did not enjoy reading this story, I hope one can at least appreciate the effort that I went through to get this photograph!

If it's mental stimulation you are after, there are things like Toastmasters. For those who are not familiar with Toastmasters, it is a worldwide organisation that helps people improve their communication skills in public speaking. It is great fun and a wonderful way to meet other English speakers. To find a club near your city or town in South Korea, go to http://www.toastmasters.org. Another website to look at is http://www.meetup.com for other social groups available in South Korea.

For those that just want to relax, there are spas available. There are also many foreigners who offer yoga classes and all you need to do is search the Facebook groups in Korea or ask a fellow native English speaker. Other leisurely activities include going to venues that have batting cages, where you can practise your baseball swing. There are also places that cater for the golfer. You can practise your golf swing by hitting your golf ball into these huge nets. Tenpin bowling is another popular activity in South Korea.

For the slightly energetic, you might want to consider Hash House Harriers. These groups are made up of predominantly English speaking foreigners. They are a worldwide organisation and you will definitely find them in Korea. Hash House Harriers are a group of runners that get together for a run and socialise afterwards. It doesn't really matter if you're a slow runner or fast runner, they cater for everyone and the emphasis is on having fun. In fact, I am not sure whether you'd call them a "running club with a drinking problem" or a "drinking club with a running problem." To find a local Hash House Harriers club in Korea, go to their website at http://gotothehash.net/korea

If you are the more active type, there are loads of activities that you can do to keep fit and also meet other English foreigners at the same time. Recreational activities like hiking and cycling are very popular in Korea. As mentioned in an earlier chapter of this book, Korea is a mountainous country. It doesn't really matter where you live in Korea, you will always be a short distance away from somewhere to hike. Should you choose to want to go and live in a rural area, there is nothing better than exploring your surrounding area on a bicycle. Unless you're an avid cyclist and have to have the top of the range bicycle, there is no need to bring your bike with you from your home country. I bought a local bicycle for about W100 000 and it had all the basics and was more than sufficient for me to cycle around town and surrounding areas. Gyms are plentiful in Korea and if there are foreigners in your town or city, you will be bound to bump into them at the gym. Their gym membership works similar to that in the West. You can pay monthly or for a few months in advance. The more months you pay for in advance, the bigger your discount. However, if you don't ask you won't get and remember, whatever price they suggest try and negotiate a little more. Prices will vary from gym to gym and dependent on what facilities they offer. I paid for six months in advance and worked out to W70 000 per month. The normal monthly rate was W100 000. Not all gyms will have indoor swimming pools. If you like to do a swimming workout your best bet would be to ask your co-teacher where the students go to practise their swimming. The pool owners may have some sort of reciprocal agreement with the local education department and maybe you'll be able to get a discount as a teacher. If being in an indoor gym isn't for you, you could also try and meet up with other foreigners in the many open parks. These open parks consist of a badminton court/s, as well as gym equipment. The gym equipment doesn't make use of weights like the standard gym equipment in gyms, but rather uses the person's own body weight. There are different machines that will work different muscle groups for you. The good news is that these parks are free and are open to the general public. If you can play badminton, table tennis, baseball or soccer you will always have someone to socialise with, as these are the most popular sports in South Korea.

One sport that deserves a separate mention is Taekwondo. Taekwondo is a type of traditional Korean martial art. "Tae" means to kick or jump. "Kwon" means a fist. "Do" means discipline. They say it is a good sport for training one's mind as well as body. It is acknowledged as an international sport and has been part of the Olympic Games since 2000. It is no surprise then that Korea won a gold medal in Taekwondo at the Beijing Olympics in 2008. It is an ideal opportunity for you to learn this sport from the masters themselves and you will find numerous schools throughout Korea. Tuition fees can vary, but in my town the average cost was around W25 000 per lesson.

The Naked Truth about Gyms

It has been six months since I last ran. It's true. I have been back in South Korea for six months now and have not run since the Two Oceans ultra marathon. I suppose it's not for a lack of not wanting to, but it's a little more difficult when you're living in a small town and you're restricted to one or two routes. Not to mention the extremes in weather. In summer, it's hot and extremely humid. In winter, not much rain, but freezing cold. It is only recently that I have discovered that it's been so long since I last ran. I was doing laundry of all things. In the nineteen months that I have been in Korea, my clothes have never shrunk. Who would have thought that clothes would have a certain life span and then all of a sudden they shrink and the next thing you know you can't fasten the button on your pants. This is where a belt is no longer an accessory, but becomes a necessity – to hide the undone button and partly opened fly. After unsuccessful enquiries into the possibilities of getting a beer belly brace, I decided I needed to join a gym to lose weight. Just in case you're wondering, a beer belly brace would probably be the equivalent of a women's sports bra. The belly brace prevents your beer belly from hitting you in the eye while you run. Looking at the various gyms in my town was certainly an eye opening experience. It wasn't quite what I was used to, but I managed to find one that would cater for my needs.

The gyms are fairly similar to Western gyms, but with a few subtle differences. You would probably need to go to the bigger cities to find a gym that has a pool, spinning classes, aerobics, etc. And having a sauna, well that's just an extra perk. Let me just give you a quick rundown of the gym that I joined for the monthly membership fee of W70 000. First of all, you get given a permanent locker the size of a mailbox. This is for your gym shoes and is located next to the workout area. The changing rooms and the workout area are on different floors, so this means that you have to take an extra pair of shoes with you. Once you've changed into your gym clothes, you need to get from the change room to the workout area where your gym shoes are. The other bonus is that you don't have to take your own towel or even toiletries. As you walk into the workout area, there is a huge stack of towels and all you have to do is help yourself. The same when you get to the showers.

The only problem with these towels is the size. They are the size of hand towels and your immediate reaction is to grab a few. However, there is no need, as they also provide these wonderful absorption types of towels. I'm sure you've seen them before. They are the ones on the TV infomercials. You know the ones...they throw one of these towels into a pool and all of a sudden all the water disappears...they then squeeze the towel out and all the water fills the pool again. Yep, those are the ones.

Now I mentioned toiletries as well. All of the soap dishes have a communal soap in them. Now I'm not talking about the liquid kind. It is actual bars of soap that everyone uses. I'm not too keen on using them and rather bring my own. I know most Korean men have black hair, but I have yet to see a Korean with short black curly hair. This is not the reason why I don't use the soap I just prefer my own brand. Call me brand loyal if you must. As for the communal hair brushes, well enough said. The other thing that strikes me as unusual is that people also leave their toothbrushes there. Nothing really wrong with that I suppose. I don't know if I would be keen to do that. Can you imagine the cleaner is busy cleaning the toilets and he is trying to clean in one of those hard to reach places...you must admit the temptation to grab the nearest handy toothbrush to help out must be overwhelmingly. Now I know some of you are probably saying a cleaner wouldn't do that and I should give them the benefit of the doubt. But let me tell you a little story about my first encounter with one of the gym personnel. When it comes to nudity there are some unwritten laws. Apparently, these laws are not applicable in Korea. I had just finished a workout and made my way down to the showers. I grabbed one of those towels that look like a mouse's duvet and made my way into the showers. There standing in front of me was one of the gym personnel, with nothing on but a pair of green Wellington boots and holding a mop grinning from ear to ear. People have told me why some farmers wear Wellington boots – they put the hind legs of the sheep in them, so that the sheep can't run away while they have their way with them. So you can imagine the look of concern I had on my face when I saw this gentleman 'dressed' the way he was. I mean what do you say to avoid confrontation with this person, "The colour of your boots matches your eyes?" I think not! Why can't he be like other cleaners and do his job fully clothed?

One would think that after this encounter you'd make a hurried exit back to the safety of the change room. However, this was just like in the movies where the killer gets shot and then the unsuspecting victim goes over to investigate to see if they are still alive. Then to the victim's horror the killer is alive, grabs them and the whole drama starts over again. So things didn't stop there for me. I decided to go into the sauna for the first time. The sauna can probably seat about six people comfortably. So there I was huddled with a group of naked men in a sauna. Yet, while I was sitting on the bench, this one guy decides to get up, face me and start doing Jack Knives without warning. I mean for goodness' sake! Besides the emotional trauma and psychological scarring this visual had caused me, didn't his mother ever teach him any manners? After all, it's rude to point! Koreans are also virtually hairless, with the exception of hair on their heads, under their arms and in the nether regions. The humorous adage, "You scratch my back, I comb yours," would be lost on them. Being a Westerner with hair on my arms and legs has caused much amazement, curiosity and 'staring' in the change room. I have even had people come up to me wanting to feel my "fur"!

A peculiar habit that some of the men seem to observe, is that of drying their nether regions with a hairdryer. And it's not covertly done either…pretend you're drying your hair and then when no-one is looking point it down in the direction of the nether regions and then quickly back up to the head and shoulders. No sir! One leg is thrust up onto the counter, the hairdryer is pointed in the appropriate direction, and the other hand starts to briskly ruffle the nether regions in a half-hearted attempt to speed up the drying process. If I didn't know any better, I would swear they were just trying to 'play' with themselves.

So after my encounter with the nude people, have I been back? Hell no! To be honest, it has nothing to do with the people at the gym or the gym personnel. As usual I over did my first few training sessions and caught a cold. This isn't half bad, because I'm so unfit and slow, it's surprising that I caught anything. However, in the words of the Terminator, "I will be back!"

POSTAL SERVICE

"The ghastly thing about postal strikes is that after they are over, the service returns to normal" – Richard J. Needham

Sooner or later you will want to send a parcel back to your home country or maybe even receive a "care" package from loved ones back home. The Koreans are super efficient and you should have no problems with sending or receiving packages. If you do encounter problems, it will probably be from your home country's side. I have sent and received numerous packages whilst in Korea. Admittedly, the first time I tried to send a postcard to a friend back home, I encountered a major communication barrier because I did not seek the help of my co-teacher. I ended up having to draw a map of Africa and pointing to the tip of Africa to indicate South Africa. I thought it was a damn fine drawing of the African continent and don't know why they insisted on wanting to send the postcard to South America! When I mentioned, "Soccer World Cup 2010," the penny seemed to have dropped and they said they would send the postcard to Na-ma-gong (South Africa). If you are going to send or receive a letter, postcard or package, get your co-teacher to write the addresses in Korean. You can then put both English and Korean addresses on and this will speed up the process of delivery. If someone is going to send you something, forward them the English and Korean address so that they too can put both addresses on the letter or package.

It is very easy and quite cheap to send a package back to your home country. The post office will also supply you with the relevant size cardboard box that you require, as well as the duct tape to seal the box. The cardboard boxes are inexpensive and will cost you a few thousand won. The process is as follows. Go into the post office and select the size cardboard box that you require. Pack whatever it is your sending home, into the box. Then seal the box with the tape provided and take to the service counter for weighing. You are then required to fill out a customs declaration form. You will pay a fee according to the weight of the package (see post office website for details). The post office official will give you a copy of the declaration form with a tracking number on it. You will be able to track the progress of your package by going to the post office website and entering the tracking number. Before leaving the post office, make sure they have used the correct country code for the package destination. If I did not double check the country code when I sent my first package home, it would have ended up in New Zealand instead of South Africa!

The post offices are open from 09h00 till 18h00 Monday to Fridays. They are closed on Saturdays, Sundays and National holidays. For information on their services and pricing go to http://www.koreapost.go.kr/eng/service

NORTH vs. SOUTH

"There never was a good war or a bad peace." – Benjamin Franklin

Over the years there has always been, what the media call "political posturing," between North Korea and South Korea. This year has been no exception, except that people are losing their lives. On 26th March 2010, South Korea accused North Korea of torpedoing a South Korean Cheonan corvette navy warship, which killed forty six sailors. South Korea reduced trade with North Korea and denied North Korean cargo ships permission to pass through their waters. North Korea retaliated by saying that it would sever ties with South Korea until 2013 when the current president leaves office. On 23rd November 2010, North Korea launched an artillery attack on Yeonpyeong Island, killing four South Koreans.

I don't mention these incidents to frighten you or to cast doubts on whether you should go to Korea or not. I'm merely making you aware of the reality of what is happening. Whenever these incidents happen, we as foreigners tend to get a little edgy. My bit of advice is to take your cue from the locals. If they seem relaxed or are not bothered about the situation, then neither should you be. I'm not for a minute suggesting that you should just play it by ear and see what happens. On the contrary, I think it is important that you register with your embassy or consulate shortly after your arrival in Korea. After all, the purpose of doing this is for security and assistance during emergencies. I would also enquire as to what action plans they have in place for evacuations in cases of emergencies. There is also no harm in linking up with other foreigners and taking the initiative to have a B-plan. I recommend that you also monitor your embassies or consulates website for updates on the situation between North and South Korea. So hopefully now you feel a little more at ease. Now go and teach! Here is a list of embassies and consulates in order for you to go and register in South Korea.

Embassy	Website	Contact
Australia	http://www.southkorea.embassy.gov.au	(02) 2003 0100
Canada	http://www.korea.gc.ca	(02) 3783 6000
Ireland	http://www.irelandhouse-korea.com	(02) 774 6455
New Zealand	http://www.nzembassy.com	(02) 3701 7700
South Africa	http://www.southafrica-embassy.or.kr	(02) 792 4855
UK	http://www.britishembassy.or.kr	(02) 3210 5500
U.S.A	http://www.seoul.usembassy.gov	(02) 397 4114

A local market

CHAPTER 6

AND IN CONCLUSION

THE GOOD, THE BAD AND THE UGLY

"Life is full of ups and downs and twists and turns. The trick is to enjoy the ups and have courage during the downs." – Author Unknown

Every culture and country has its pros and cons. It is no different in South Korea. Your time there can be good; it can be bad; it can be ugly or all three. You can ask any foreign teacher about their experiences in Korea and they may tell you about experiences similar to mine. Although, there might also be other foreign teachers who have worked in Korea and have not experienced what I have experienced. In fact, they could have experienced totally the opposite. Even if you end up teaching at multiple schools, you will also realise that each school has its own unique personality. Everyone's experience will be unique to them. It's is entirely up to you as to what you do and make of that experience. If you are set in your ways and are unaccommodating, your stay in Korea could be less than easy. A worthwhile caveat to keep in mind is, "Expect the unexpected." The key here is to be reasonably flexible and having an attitude of taking each day as it comes.

Your school will want you to not only teach your students English, but a little about your country's culture as well. I recommend that you be a cultural ambassador in front of your students, but refrain from trying to force your culture onto your Korean colleagues or other Koreans outside of the workplace. If you are willing to learn, accept and understand their culture, you will truly experience Korean friendship and a sense of belonging. I went to South Korea with the intention of teaching, but I can assure you that I also ended up being taught, learning and growing as I went along.

Whether you are a teacher by profession or not, everyone will have something of value to teach in which their students will be able to profit from. There is no right or wrong teaching persona. Each will be unique and one must be comfortable with that and not try and emulate someone else. Bring your creativity, enthusiasm and energy. You will find that it will be contagious and be picked up by your students in your classroom. Other than that, all that is required of you is to do the best you can. Remember, as the Japanese proverb goes, "Better than a thousand days of diligent study is one day with a great teacher."

Above all, remember that it is not your right to teach in South Korea, it's your privilege! Being a TEFL teacher in Korea brings important responsibilities and opportunities. There is an expectation that we will come with fresh, fun and exciting ways of teaching English to students. However, some foreigners have gone over to South Korea with the thinking that they are going to change the system and that the way things are done in the West are the only way things should be done. I can assure you that this type of arrogance will only be met with a "stand offish" kind of behaviour from your colleagues and the potential of them not liking you. This will obviously impact on how easy or difficult your time will be in South Korea. Therefore, it is important to be aware of this and work at cultivating your relationship with your work colleagues, especially your co-teachers.

Regrets, I have had a few, but then again too few to mention

Today, I finished doing four weeks of Winter English camps. We worked straight through Christmas and New Year, so not much time for reflection and contemplation of events over the last year. I'm just so relieved that the camps are over. I feel like doing what Mel Gibson did in Brave Heart, painting my face blue and running outside, thrusting my hands into the air and shouting, "Freedom!" I now have five days off to cast my mind back over the last year.

Two years ago when I was thinking about going to a foreign country to experience a different culture, many people said that it was an experience of a lifetime and that I should go for it. Of course, what about ninety percent of the people conveniently forgot to mention to me, was that they had never done it themselves.

Needless to say, taking their advice into consideration and equipped with English expressions like, "Fortune favours the brave," to bolster my confidence, I took the plunge and here we are two years later. It was an experience of a lifetime indeed. When someone mentions that to you, it conjures up images of excitement and adventure. However, it's not all excitement, adventure and plain sailing. There are occasions where things do get a little rough and tough. But I suppose that is all part of the experience...the good and the bad. And I have had my fair share of both those experiences while I have been in South Korea.

They say you always remember your first time and trust me, I remember the first time I suffered from culture shock while in Korea. It's etched in my mind. I don't think I will ever be able to forget the whole going to the toilet story. I'm over the fact that most public toilets consist of basically a hole in the ground surrounded by what one can only describe as a baby's potty and then you have to squat over this while doing your 'business.' What freaks me out is the toilet paper story. In Korea, you don't flush the toilet paper down the toilet you place it in a basket next to the toilet. I know you are probably wondering how they dispose of it once the basket is full and so have I. I have not asked and have no intention of asking. It's a precautionary measure. Just in case they tell me it is recycled and then sold as toilet paper again. It will just freak me out all over again and cause more psychological scarring!

Recently I was on an internet social networking site in one of the groups related to teaching in South Korea. There was this one person who had been in Korea for a few months posting the odd comment. Their comments were always of a negative nature. If they did have something positive to say, they would always follow it up with many other negative comments. It's almost as if they relished the opportunity for someone to post something, so that they could make a negative comment about it. I have chatted to this person many times and they are the same in person. I've actually wondered why they even bothered to stay here as long as they have. I feel sorry for the poor person who is considering teaching English in Korea and reads their comments. I'm sure they will have second thoughts about coming to Korea. However, I feel people like them and the type of experiences they have had, are in the minority.

One person posted a comment about teaching English in a foreign country. He said he was a bit nervous and had doubts about signing the contract and coming over. He asked fellow users of the group the following question, "Do you think I should do it or not?" Various people came back with advice for him, but one piece of advice really stuck out. I thought the advice this person had given was not only appropriate for this situation, but pretty much any situation that you've thoroughly researched and are hesitant about. He asked the person to consider this, "How many things have you done in your life that you have regretted? How many things have you not done in your life that you have regretted?" Chances are if you are like most of us, the things you regret the most are probably the things you have not done. We spend a lot of our time wishing that we had done something. We rarely regret the things we have done. The bottom line is that this guy was suggesting that he go for it, because if he didn't, he would probably regret it more than if he did. The person with all their negative comments is probably so wrapped up in their negativity that they failed to see the opportunity that lay in front of them. Admittedly, coming from the West to the East is a huge culture shock for anyone. Nothing can really prepare you for it no matter how much research you do. This situation and the fact that my contract is coming up for renewal, got me thinking, "Have I got any regrets?"

In my first year here, it was like being on a rollercoaster. One minute you're having a wonderful time and on an absolute high, then the next minute you are at the other end of the spectrum and start thinking to yourself, "What the hell made me decide to sign-up for this." It can go on like that for days, even months, but once you stop taking things *personally and just become flexible and go with the flow, it becomes so much easier. Initially, what caused most of my frustration was trying to do and control things the way we would do and control them in a Western society. After numerous occasions of hitting my head against a brick wall, I started to do things the way the Koreans did them. Things became a little less stressful. I suppose the old adage, "When in Rome do as the Romans do," has some truth to it. There have been some rough times while I have been here, but I have always managed to come through them. In hindsight, I have also learnt so much, not only about myself, but about people in general. The Koreans, just like any other nationality, have their good things and their not so good things, but nevertheless they have taught me a lot about friendship, generosity, compassion and a sense of community. In my mind, these things are well worth learning about. So I suppose it really depends on your attitude and how flexible you are prepared to be in order to fit in here. Do I have any regrets? I think I will let Frank Sinatra do my talking for me. "Regrets, I have had a few, but then again too few to mention. I did what I had to do. And saw it through without exemption. Yes, there were times, I'm sure you knew when I bit off more than I could chew. But through it all, when there was doubt, I ate it up and spit it out. I faced it all and I stood tall, and did it my way."*

LETTERS FROM AFAR

"Goodbyes are not forever. Goodbyes are not the end. They simply mean I'll miss you until we meet again." - Author Unknown

You build up such an incredible relationship with your school, especially the students. You are able to witness how their personalities develop, while at the same time watching how they grow in confidence when learning the English language. There is a saying, "All good things must come to an end" and probably the worst part of the job is having to say goodbye. I was advised that I had to give a farewell speech to all the teachers and staff. The speech was much longer than my introduction speech and I had managed to get my co-teacher to translate it into Korean for me. It was quite an emotional speech and had numerous teachers in tears. The Koreans sharing, generosity and kindness that I had come to know, came to the fore again that day when I was given many farewell gifts from teachers and staff alike. I was fortunate enough to be able to have dinner with all four of my co-teachers on my last night in Korea. Koreans have this belief that the family is always more important than the individual. It really felt that I wasn't just leaving a job, but that I was leaving behind family. You build up such a close friendship. At dinner, one of my co-teachers asked her colleague if she would change seats with her. She wanted to sit next to me as this would be the last time that she would be able to. I hope and trust that as a foreign English teacher in Korea you get to experience this type of friendship and concept of being part of a family. Furthermore, on my last day of teaching I was inundated with letters from students. It would not be practical to place all the letters in this book, so I have selected a few which will hopefully convey to you the warmth and character of the type of students you are likely to encounter in South Korea.

And in conclusion...in the words of so many of my students that I taught in South Korea, "Have a good time. See you later."

Teacher Alain,

I've heard you're leaving this week. I guess today is your last day of our school. I'm ▓▓▓▓ in 3rd grade, 1st class. Maybe you might remember me. I've once attended your English Conversation class (After school) when I was 1st grade. My hair is very long (I'm not sure you've seen my long hair. I usually pony tail it ☺). This can be a clue to remember me. Actually, my hair is super long ☺ I've never been to South Africa. I really want to visit their during 2012 world cup. Stay healthy and always be happy there. Oh, I was surprised that you run full course marathon. I heard ▓▓▓▓ teacher prepared a pair of sneakers for your hobby. Please keep my short letter ~☺ Keep in touch!!!

P.S. Don't forget our school!!!
If you forget, I'll cry~ ☺
I'll miss you ~ ☹

To. Alain,
Hello! My name is
████████ !!
I'm Sad. Becaus You leave in Korea....
You are very kind & fun!! You know? ^^*
I'll miss you forever ♡
In Vacation I was studied with you.
Do you remembeh? ㅠㅠ
I want you don't forget me.
And Have a good trip..
Let's meet next next next Year!! ><
Good Bye

Dear. Alain howes..

Hello., I'm ▮▮▮▮ in ▮▮▮ Middle School.
I'm sad that you go now.
I hope I can meet you again Someday in the future.
don't forget about Korea and Korean people including myself.
I will miss you..

Dear. Alain Teacher

Hello Alain! My name is ▮▮▮▮▮ I'm 3-1 class.
I'm so sad when I heard that you will leave. But I
believe, may be we can meet someday!
   Alain, You're good teacher. when I met you first, You
are very very kind Also I am sorry about the last winter
vacation. I absent the class. please forgive me.
   Teacher, I heard that You will study in your country.
I will cheer up for you! Ha Ha.. please understand my
grammar ability... I will study English more hard then
I will visit The South Africa.
         Then please remember me! I will miss you
      and remember you! good-bye Alain.

P.S: I will email you someday!
Mine: ▮▮▮▮▮▮▮▮▮▮

cheer up!
Good-Bye

ALAIN

Hello! I am ▮▮▮▮
I'm a student of ▮▮▮▮ middle school. I remember your first face vivid. when I was first grade (last last year) I feel special Because your English is different with I have known. I have learned English about America's and your's is England's But I feel interesting in your class because I can learn new things. I am thanks for your teaching and I'll never forget you Please remember Hankook (korea) and Bu chun middle school. I hope you have good memory about korea. It's time for say good bye... I heard your news I feel sad. I'll miss you. Thank you! ^^
At the South Africa you have good health and good... everything is good. Good bye~
Forever happy & smile ~ ☺

Disclaimer:

Whilst writing this book I was heavily under the influence of drinking gold Korean red ginseng tea with the sounds of Arirang blaring in my ear. Any references of favouritism and patriotism towards South Korea are purely co-incidental.